P
Fall a

"A memoir of strength, persistence, and—most of all—love. Parenting is never easy, but, as De Simone discovers, raising two children with disabilities can easily knock a mother down. Gracefully weaving the threads of dance, motherhood, and disability through her remarkable journey, De Simone shows us all how to 'fall with the direct intention to rise.'"

—KAREN DEBONIS, author of *Growth: A Mother, Her Son, and the Brain Tumor They Survived*

"Heartfelt and engaging, this memoir of raising children requiring vastly varying degrees of care and advocacy delicately threads blurred, complicated, and demanding lines. With the best parts of quiet compassion, noiseless rage, and complete, unconditional acceptance, Joanne De Simone depicts a specific, sweeping motherhood that soars far above unrelenting daily demands. Through the lens of her foundation in dance, Joanne embraces the gift of the children in her home, not those who once occupied her imagination."

—LISA ROMEO, author of *Starting With Goodbye: A Daughter's Memoir of Love After Loss*

"The Limón technique centers the defined poles of 'fall' and 'recovery.' However, the *dance* is what happens in the undefined, unpredictable, unsettled, and magnificently alive moment-to-moment between the two. Wholly embodying this in-between mercurial time/space, Joanne De Simone writes—as she danced, as she lives—with raw honesty, brilliance, and seemingly boundless generosity. Joanne's is a fierce grace; not delicately poised above, but rather in a visceral and dynamic intimacy with the gravity, heartfelt vulnerability, and wonder of person and parenthood."

—Steuart Gold, somatic psychotherapist
and former Limón Company dancer

"Joanne vividly paints a picture of the dance that you must learn when parenting children with medically complex and neuro-diverse needs. This book challenges service providers to be a compassionate light in the darkness while also inspiring parents navigating a life unplanned yet beautiful in its design."

—Aubrey Schmalle, OTR/L, speaker, author,
and owner of Sensational Achievements, LLC

"Rarely does someone convey the experience of raising a child with a disability with such beauty and honesty. Joanne De Simone has managed to raise not one but two children with dignity, respect, and a drive to make certain that the world will be a better place for them because of her tireless love, advocacy, and activism. A must-read for families with challenges, as well as anyone who craves others' authenticity to help process the pain and joy life offers us."

—Alma Schneider, LCSW, cofounder of
the *2 Moms No Fluff* podcast and
cofounder of 1in6 Consulting Foundation

Fall *and* Recovery

Fall *and* Recovery

RAISING CHILDREN WITH
DISABILITIES THROUGH
LESSONS LEARNED IN DANCE

Joanne De Simone

SHE WRITES PRESS

Published 2024

Printed in the United States of America

Print ISBN: 978-1-64742-714-6
E-ISBN: 978-1-64742-715-3
Library of Congress Control Number: 2024904178

For information, address:
She Writes Press
1569 Solano Ave #546
Berkeley, CA 94707

Interior design and typeset by Katherine Lloyd, The DESK

She Writes Press is a division of SparkPoint Studio, LLC.

Portions of this book previously appeared as "Benjamin Is Benjamin" by Joanne De Simone in *Barriers and Belonging: Personal Narratives of Disability* edited by Michelle Jarman, Leila Monaghan, and Alison Quaggin Harkin. Used by permission of Temple University Press. © 2017 by Temple University. All Rights Reserved.

Some portions of this book were first published in *Brain, Child* magazine, *Literary Mama*, the *Huffington Post*, the *Mighty*, and the *Rumpus*.

For Benjamin and Sebastian

In memory of John Palamara and Jim Clinton

To every thing there is a season,
and a time to every purpose under the heaven:

A time to be born, and a time to die; a time to plant,
and a time to pluck up that which is planted;

A time to kill, and a time to heal; a time to break down,
and a time to build up;

A time to weep, and a time to laugh; a time to mourn,
and a time to dance;

A time to cast away stones, and a time to gather stones together;
a time to embrace, and a time to refrain from embracing;

A time to get, and a time to lose; a time to keep,
and a time to cast away;

A time to rend, and a time to sew; a time to keep silence,
and a time to speak;

A time to love, and a time to hate; a time of war,
and a time of peace.

—Ecclesiastes 3: 1–8 KJV

Contents

Part Three:
Connecting through Space *and* Time

Author's Note

This memoir is filled with stories of my life from my perspective. I studied the Limón dance technique for over two years with at least a dozen teachers. Unless otherwise noted, the dance lessons described in this book come from those collective years and instructors.

Some names and characteristics have been changed in order to protect identities.

This book covers my experiences up until 2016, when my sons were seventeen and thirteen years old. Information regarding special education laws and disability services may be different at the time of publication. Medical decisions and educational strategies discussed in this manuscript are not presented as advice. Please seek information and assistance from trained medical and educational professionals.

Preface

I have a confession to make: ableism negatively influenced my experiences as a mother.

I didn't realize this for many years. As a parent, I didn't acknowledge the subtle and not-so-subtle messages our culture steeps us in. For me, ableism drives the awful hierarchy we live within—one where people are valued based on their cognitive intelligence and physical capabilities. I still encounter strangers who take one look at my son Benjamin in his wheelchair and say, "I'm sorry." As a parent, I have wrestled with and will continue to work on subduing the internalized belief that having a disabled child is bad.

I remember when doctors blamed mothers for their child's autism, deeming them cold "refrigerator moms." While we now know this is false, I believe these types of lies live in our culture's subconscious. Many are buried, and some have even been forgotten, but they're still there. In all my years of education, I was never taught the full history of how the disabled have been viewed and mistreated. I am still learning.

As an expectant mother, I was offered genetic testing and the opportunity to terminate the pregnancy if abnormalities were detected. I know mothers who refused the option to abort. Some were told that making the conscious decision to bring a disabled child into the world would ruin their lives. I never heard those exact words, but the message was clear and lived within me. I now recognize the myths I bought into, like the belief that having disabled children was a punishment. My version of motherhood brought conflict. I spent years simultaneously loving my sons and grieving their situations as a result of the negative attitudes that were passed down throughout history.

As a special educator, I relied heavily on educational and medical models that seemed to reinforce the idea that my children's disabilities were my doing and that their existence would always place our family in a state of being unwanted and unwelcome—not by our families, not by the majority of our friends, but by the world in which I will one day be forced to leave my children behind, a world where disabled children didn't have the right to an education until 1975, a world where many children are still educated in segregated classrooms, a world where some children sit home alone because they are never invited to playdates, a world where the disabled are grossly unemployed or underemployed. I experienced a very real sense of isolation as a parent of disabled children. Acknowledging ableism wasn't enough to successfully navigate this isolation.

This story is an uncensored tour of my heart, my soul, and the inner thoughts I struggled with as a result of how ableism (as I later came to appreciate) informed and guided me as a mother. I divulge ugly truths. I say things that some parents choose to keep hidden for fear that no one will understand. I wrote this book so parents of disabled children will feel less isolated by their darkest thoughts and to encourage a release of all the shame that comes with them.

It's easy to say that a large part of my struggle as a parent of disabled children is because of ableism, but I think that is an oversimplification. It will always be painful for me to watch Benjamin have a seizure. It hurts me to see him in pain, and it hurts me to feel helpless in the face of that pain, to the point that I fall into the trap of blaming myself for it. Human beings are complicated, and I believe the only way to learn and understand each other better is by sharing true stories.

Some argue that describing these struggles has the potential to further ableism. I'd like to live in a world where parents don't experience pain, grief, anxiety, and depression, but we're not there yet. Perhaps this book can be used to prove why ableist attitudes must change.

My sons are wonderful human beings. They have always been wonderful human beings. I continue the journey of living up to the example they set for me.

Part One

Disconnected

Don't Break the Circle

To every thing there is a season

Time began in darkness. In the spring of 1988, I stood center stage with twelve other Hunter College Dance Company members ready to perform José Limón's classic dance, *There Is a Time*, based on Chapter 3 in the book of Ecclesiastes.

Taking slow breaths, I felt the natural rise as the cool stage air expanded my body beyond its physical barriers and the inevitable fall leaving me both lengthened and grounded. I gave a gentle squeeze to the dancers holding my hands and imagined the single large circle we'd maintain for *Time's* opening section. The first quiet, sustained high note arrived. We stood still as four bars of strings played above it. Then silence. The lights ascended. We inhaled together as the music began again with a deeper, somber melody. We exhaled and swayed side to side.

Music and breath guided us through subtle shoulder rotations and lilting side bends. Sweaty hands made accommodations but held firm. The next inhalation widened our arms, expanding the circle to maximum capacity. With an exhalation, we lunged forward and tightened the orb. In unison our torsos bent forward, sideward, and lengthened back. Shoulders, elbows, and wrists rotated, creased, and flexed. Connected as one, we traveled around with quick, petite steps swooping into lyrical leg swings. We bowed to the circle's empty center and looked up to the heavens.

Jim Clinton, my mentor and accomplished soloist with the Limón Company, had instructed us: "Circles are *Time's* choreographic motif. They represent time and a timeless oneness with others. Without them, we lose a belief in community and the ability to share life's joys and struggles. Whatever you do, don't break the circle."

In practical terms, a break in the circle would not only destroy the illusion Limón's dance created but would send us all flying off in a manner from which there could be no graceful recovery. In rehearsal, the image of a ring-around-the-rosie game gone awry was comical, but there's nothing funny about losing a vital connection, flailing through space fighting to recapture a bond, and crashing toward the middle of nowhere like debris from a tornado.

This story begins with Benjamin. Every hardship I had endured up until his birth in 1999 set the stage for motherhood, and everything finally seemed perfect. I couldn't have choreographed the first week of parenthood any better. Sleep deprivation wasn't bothering me a bit. Nor were the mounds of laundry or a house overrun by baby gear. Benjamin cried only when he was hungry, and we quickly mastered breastfeeding. My husband kept notes on Benjamin's nursing schedule and made light of the messy world of diaper duty, declaring, "He's the lord of the dump." John looked at Benjamin with a depth of love and hope I hadn't anticipated. Flooded with the most positive postpartum hormones, I felt an unbreakable connection to this family circle. I was certain the massive changes that threaten to unravel otherwise happy couples wouldn't faze us. We finally had a baby in our arms. Nothing else mattered. Then we went for Benjamin's one-week checkup.

Don't Break the Circle

The pediatrician placed the measuring tape around Benjamin's head and noted, "His head size is a little small, but your head size is a little small." That was it. The seeds of doubt and despair took root. Dr. Gabriel thought everything else seemed fine. Benjamin was eating, sleeping, and pooping. What else does a one-week-old do? As I dressed my baby boy, the doctor led John to the consultation room where he began, "I hope I didn't insult your wife with my comment about her head size."

John assured him, "No." He was right. I wasn't insulted, but neither of them realized I was growing a plantation of fear.

As we passed the next few weeks, I worked hard to suppress my anxiety. *Come on, Joanne, Benjamin is fine. Look at how he stares into your eyes forever. He's pure love, and how cute is he with his George Clooney hairstyle? Every strand perfectly placed. You should know better than to act like some paranoid, first-time mother after twelve years of teaching gymnastics and three years as a preschool special education teacher.*

At Benjamin's two-month-old checkup, his head was indeed still too small, and the soft spot on the top of his head appeared to be closing. As we waited for an appointment with a pediatric neurologist, Benjamin's head size became an obsession. We kept a measuring tape in his changing table among the diapers, wipes, and butt cream and measured his head regularly as if the tape would somehow defy the truth.

Our first consultation with the neurologist revealed that Benjamin's development appeared normal. I answered some basic questions about my pregnancy. "Yes, my alpha-fetoprotein blood test was abnormal. Yes, we went to genetic counseling and learned we had roughly a one percent chance of there being an abnormality. Yes, I had a normal amniocentesis." We left only with instructions to return in two months, but the neurologist's words haunted me. "Perhaps Benjamin was trying to tell you something with that AFP result."

A rude, evil little voice hovered around me whispering, *Something's wrong.* My friends talked about the changes their babies were making from week to week. Benjamin stopped following the developmental charts. I didn't share my observations with John. If I didn't speak the words, perhaps there was still a chance to deny reality. I kept checking the parenting books. Benjamin was smiling and tracking toys with his eyes, but he wasn't finding his hands. Early on, I had asked the pediatrician, "How long do we have to sterilize everything?"

He replied, "Until he starts putting his fingers in his mouth." Now I wondered exactly when that would be.

At Benjamin's baptism, I stood in a pew behind three rows of mothers with their little ones propped up over their shoulders. I smiled at all those little faces looking at me. All those babies picking up their heads to greet me. I hugged Benjamin tight up against my own shoulder. I swayed side to side with those parents to a similar cadence, but Benjamin was only able to bobble his head with an uncoordinated kind of motion. I gave him extra support when taking pictures with the priest. I smiled and tried to comfort myself with the disclaimer that every child develops at a different rate.

When Benjamin was four months old, the neurologist harvested my fears. In a narrow, gray, and otherwise unmemorable office, she performed the standard test for head lag. Benjamin was lying on his back. The doctor pulled him by his arms. He still didn't have the ability to hold up his own head, but eventually gravity helped him to jerk it forward. His head flop didn't jar me, but the position of his body did. Most babies end sitting up. The doctor had pulled Benjamin up like a piece of wood, straight to standing. She said, "He's hypertonic and still has a startle reflex."

Babies are born with some basic reflexes that are supposed to fade as their central nervous systems mature. Benjamin was still showing this Moro reflex. He'd involuntarily throw his arms out to the side and widen his eyes, as if frightened. He had quite a few exaggerated reflexes. If we passed by a window on a sunny day, Benjamin would throw his head back, stiffen his arms against his body, and squeeze his eyes closed. Ignorant of the significance of his reaction, we nicknamed him Dracula.

The doctor pronounced that it was time to start some testing. She suggested an EEG to check for brain wave abnormalities, an MRI for structural abnormalities, blood work for organic acid abnormalities. As we questioned the rationale for each test, she began a bizarre banter: "The brain is like a cake. It might look good on the outside, but how does it taste? You don't know until you cut it open and taste it." I was speechless. *Are you seriously comparing my son's brain to a cake?*

Then she offered the phone number to call for early intervention services. I froze at the sheer mention of it. From the one early intervention course I had taken while studying for my master's in special education, I knew the younger a child was identified, the more severe their diagnosis. I questioned her: "Why call for early intervention before we've done any testing?"

She simply said, "Starting occupational and physical therapies won't hurt."

As we walked out of the building, John asked me, "Why are you so upset about the thought of calling for services?"

I told him the only thing I was certain of. "If she can tell at age four months, without testing, that he needs therapy, something is catastrophically wrong with Benjamin."

As we arranged appointments for Benjamin's tests, John grew increasingly pessimistic. One night, while passing me in the hallway, he said, "Benjamin is going to be retarded, and we will end up divorced." His language was jarring. It froze me. The use of hurtful labels and the message of divorce were unnerving. After nearly six years of marriage, it wasn't a fear I'd entertained, but my studies at Hunter supported higher divorce rates among couples with children with disabilities. I hated the idea of being another statistic, and such an obvious one at that.

Whenever I'm scared or filled with uncertainty, I remind myself of the hardships I've lived through. I started this practice when my father died two weeks shy of my ninth birthday. I can still see my brother, hours from his nuptials, hovering over our father administering chest compressions. I always believed I could survive anything after that. This mindset came in handy when the director of the José Limón Company called to say she'd chosen a different dancer to fill the one rare open spot I'd auditioned for.

John sat with me as I received the rejection. We had just returned to his parents' house after burying his father. Working hard to steady my voice, I squeezed John's hand a little tighter and said goodbye to her. Wanting to absorb my pain, John licked my tears and we cried together. Where was that bond now? I stood alone in the hallway between our bedroom and Benjamin's wondering if we could withstand this whirlwind. I felt our once unbreakable family circle slipping from my grasp.

Benjamin's blood work and EEG were normal. The MRI proved to be a challenge from the start. Benjamin needed an IV sedation in order to perform the test, which meant he had to fast. The thought of withholding nourishment from a four-month-old was both physically painful because I was breastfeeding and emotionally against my Italian ancestry.

Benjamin slept through the night more soundly than I did, but by the time the three of us got to the hospital, discovered the doctor hadn't sent the orders, and failed to do so for two more hours, he was inconsolable. In a room filled with too many people restraining one small infant, the nurses attempted to start the IV. With my face inches from Benjamin's, his cries pierced me with every stick. I shot a desperate look toward John. We started singing to Benjamin, but there was no comfort.

After several tries, and a futile search for additional options, the head nurse said, "He's too dehydrated. Why don't you feed him? He's probably exhausted. Perhaps we can accomplish the MRI during his natural sleep." Typical hospital rules insisted that only one parent could stay with Benjamin in radiology. Since I had the pacifying, milk-filled breasts, John headed to the waiting room.

I cuddled up with Benjamin, and although he was furiously rooting for his too-long-awaited meal, I stopped to take a deep breath to clear my mind of the chaos and encourage my milk to flow. He latched on, quick and tight. I welcomed the relief, but the bright fluorescent lights, dingy white walls, and forced distance from John competed for my sense of peace. I looked at Benjamin's eyelids growing heavy and promised him, "This is the last test, beauty boy, and then we can go home."

The nurse gingerly wrapped him up in a blanket, strapped him onto the MRI table, and escorted me to the door. I tiptoed out, trying to keep him in sight. I stared through the glass into the darkened room and prayed. "Please let him stay asleep. Please let him be okay. Please let the results come back normal. Hail Mary, full of grace. . . ." Earlier that morning, John and I had seen a young boy whose head was narrow and oblong. He made a dark, sad impression on us. We imagined a life filled with endless uncertainty.

The testing began. All the clicking and banging of the machinery woke Benjamin. I could see him moving around. *Stay still, Benjamin.* The images were worthless. So, we repeated the whole feeding, sleeping, placing, praying, noisy, useless images cycle again. And again. Desperate to accomplish the goal of getting a look at the physical structure of his brain, the technician suggested we try a CAT scan. It would be faster and give enough detail for the time being. Benjamin got through it on the first attempt.

Fall *and* Recovery

The results came in the form of a message left on our voice-mail on a Friday afternoon. The neurologist reported, "There were several abnormalities including enlarged ventricles and pachygyria." In 1999, John and I didn't own a computer and the word *Google* had not entered mainstream vocabulary. I played the message over and over. I raced for my medical dictionary and tore through my special education textbooks. In an attempt to define everything before calling John at work, I tried to decide which of my three older brothers could help. Joseph, eighteen years my senior, has a degree in clinical psychology. John, twelve years older than me, is an X-ray tech. Or James. We are seven years apart and have the tightest emotional bond. I called James. He's medically minded, having also been an X-ray tech. As soon as I heard his voice, I jumped in, "James, do you know what *pachy-gyria* means?" He read a sketchy definition from one of his books and added, "I'll be right over."

I paced around the house trying to dissipate the sick energy whirling through my body. I practiced a tension releasing exercise I had learned as a dancer. *Squeeze your hands and arms tight, now release. Squeeze your face tight, now release.* Desperate to recapture any sense of stability, I rushed into James's arms the moment he passed through the vestibule and sobbed. "What did I do? What did I do to Benjamin? What does this mean?" The power of his embrace was strong, but the intensity of the pain we were streaming was stronger. Keeping a firm grip on my shoulders, he pulled back. His face was red, and tears accentuated his long, black eyelashes. "You did nothing wrong."

I desperately tried to call the doctor back but only reached her voicemail. As I was making another wave of calls, to John and to my best friend, Ann, who was the school psychologist at my preschool, the doctor called me back, but I missed her call. It's strange to imagine how we lived without cell phones, or even call waiting. We played a few more rounds of phone tag. I could hear the annoyance in her voice when she said, "I'll talk to you next week." I called once more, shaking as I waited for the beep. "Please, I promise I won't touch my phone again until I hear from you. You can't leave this kind of message for us on a Friday afternoon and expect us to get through the weekend." I grabbed the phone as soon as it rang, but all she said was, "I'm reading from the report and haven't seen the films yet. We can go over everything in my office at your next visit." A next visit was not what I wanted. I wanted answers.

Over the next two weeks, John and I took turns calling, asking for clarification. John told her, "The glass is already half empty. We want the truth." She made ridiculous statements such as, "When Benjamin is older and he sees an apple, will he be able to tell you it's an apple? I don't know. Benjamin is Benjamin. You should just love him." It was all nonsense. Our love was not in question. Consumed with grief and uncertainty, we continued to pursue an explanation of the findings. She snapped at me: "Mrs. De Simone, I have spent an exorbitant amount of time with you on this."

At that moment, the switch flipped in my brain, and my Brooklyn heritage emerged. "Fine," I said. Slamming the phone on the cradle, I heard my hovering whisperer say, *Don't worry, lady. You will never have to deal with me again. I am done with you.*

The Impressions section of the CAT scan report stated, "The above findings most probably represent subcategory of lissencephaly." Lissencephaly. I had never heard of it. My medical dictionary and special education textbooks failed me again. I brought the report to my pediatrician. We had barely moved away from the reception desk when he began reading it. He said, "I don't know what this is, but I'll contact some colleagues and find out." How could he not know? I couldn't breathe. Unable to balance, I leaned on the handles of Benjamin's stroller. Dr. Gabriel hustled me and Benjamin into his office, had the secretary bring me water, sat me down, and made me look at my son. Benjamin was laughing at me. He always laughed at me when I cried. Dr. Gabriel said, "See how he's looking at you? He's being so appropriate." Even though I really didn't feel any better, I accepted his genuine act of kindness. My criteria for physician conduct had been set.

Writing the name of his sister's neurologist on his prescription pad, Dr. Gabriel said, "We're done playing games. You need a real neurologist." I could barely stand the fear of the unknown. What is lissencephaly other than a diagnosis our pediatrician had never seen? What did it mean for five-month-old Benjamin?

While gathering Benjamin's test results, I decided to obtain his hospital birth records and my entire prenatal file. After listening to the initial CAT scan results left on our voicemail, I called my OB-GYN. I was hoping Dr. Mayer could help me get a grip on what was happening and why. The man had discovered and resolved my polycystic ovarian syndrome and guided us through a miscarriage. This time all he could offer was a sympathetic ear and my records. While some of our relatives pointed their fingers at him, wondering why he hadn't caught a problem during the pregnancy, my heart told me to keep my fingers to myself. I suppose it's easier to blame someone else for all the wrong in your life. I was too busy blaming myself.

John and I spent at least an hour with the new neurologist, Dr. Gold, detailing Benjamin's history. Dr. Gold examined Benjamin, looked at all the medical documents, and even asked to watch Benjamin nurse. I certainly hadn't expected to bare myself in that way, but assessing oral motor functioning seemed logical, and he stepped out of the room until Benjamin had latched on. When Dr. Gold declared, "He has a good suck," I felt I had passed some kind of motherhood test. I was proud of Benjamin for being compliant. So proud, I dropped my worries.

Dr. Gold sat behind his desk, looked us straight in the face, and said, "Well, he has cerebral palsy."

I leaned forward and repeated the words back to him. "Cerebral palsy?"

He seemed stunned. "No one told you that before?"

I was barely able to respond, "No." How could he tell that a five-month-old had cerebral palsy? My mind had already begun to numb from the sudden shift in my heart rate in response to an inability to take my next breath. An odd silence accompanied a deepening sorrow. It felt as though my brain had initiated an out-of-body experience, as a defense mechanism, so I wouldn't have that stroke I felt surely was about to happen.

Dr. Gold looked at Benjamin's hospital discharge record again. "They should have known immediately something was wrong. It says right here his head size was small for his weight and length. There's even a drawing of the abnormal shape of his head."

My mind played back moments of uncertainty from our hospital stay. During one of his first diaper changes, Benjamin turned a light shade of blue. John was so busy focusing on the diaper, he didn't notice. I yelled at him to pick Benjamin up and pat his back. I mentioned it to the staff pediatrician as he examined my son. The doctor snapped, "He's a perfectly normal, healthy baby." Why was he so defensive? The next day, a nurse came in for a routine check and in an authoritative voice instructed, "This baby should be on his side." I was too stunned to question her, but back lying was the well-advertised, recommended sleeping position to avoid SIDS. Did *she* know something? What did I miss? What did I do? Then there was the night I let Benjamin stay in the nursery. I got up confused the next morning because no one had woken me to nurse him. Hadn't they read the sign we placed in his bassinet? *No bottles or pacifiers. Breastfed only.* When I arrived at the nursery, the nurse grumbled, "He was crying all night." Was it more than just hunger?

The reel of my flashback abruptly ended when Dr. Gold unleashed a string of words I never wanted to hear. "He'll

probably never walk or talk or use his hands, but more importantly, I have no idea what his cognitive functioning will be." Just
like that, we had the explanation the first neurologist couldn't or
wouldn't give us. It was one breath of declarations immediately
and forever burned into my soul. Done, I was done. I would never
be the same. How could I possibly absorb this? How could I possibly survive this?

Benjamin was going to be more disabled than any child I had
ever worked with. Every fear I imagined actually came to life. He
was physically and intellectually disabled. It was the moment that
redefined my definition of life traumas. One percent. Didn't the
genetic counselor say we had a 1 percent chance of there being a
problem? Forget playing the lottery. We won it. We would never
beat a set of odds in our favor in our lifetime. I could feel nothing
except pain. Hear nothing except my tears as they hit the leather
chair. With my chin to my chest, I watched them drop. They
made a cold, hard sound. I can still hear the rhythm they created
and feel every sensation, like the musical score of a dance I performed long ago.

John placed his hand on my back. When I saw his tears, I
averted my gaze. It was too much. Needing a focal point, I stared
at Benjamin in total disbelief. How could this be true? Dr. Gold
looked directly into my eyes, so serious yet kind, but I couldn't
hear his words. *Did he say I reminded him of his wife? How did this
happen? Why me? Why Benjamin? Was it the fever I had the week
I conceived? Was it the cold I had early in my pregnancy? Was it the
smell of the chemicals my next-door neighbors used while renovating
their house? Was there lead in our drinking water? Is this how a nervous breakdown actually feels? How will I ever be able to look at this
baby without crying?*

Don't Limit Yourself

A time to be born, and a time to die

When the performances of *Time* were over, Jim met with us for one last class. We sat in a circle on the wooden studio floor. It was so quiet, devoid of the live musicians, sweat, and hustle of learning one of modern dance's most historic choreographic works. Jim spoke to us in his slow Mississippi cadence, looking at us through the thick lenses of his simple, wire-framed glasses. "How are y'all doing?" My body was sore from performing, and I had a nasty bruise on my left shin after falling into a speaker hidden backstage on opening night, but I felt blessed, transformed in ways I was only beginning to understand.

I'd taken a total of five classes with Jim over the course of two years. Of all the lessons he taught, I chose to ignore the one he gave that day. He said, "Don't limit yourself." Despite his warning, after graduating a semester later, I studied with the Limón Company almost exclusively for the next two years. I performed with a few smaller companies, but Limón was my one real dream. When I was invited to dance as a guest member on Limón's Eastern European *Missa Brevis* tour, I hoped I was on my way to becoming a full-fledged company member.

Perhaps it was an unrealistic dream. My dance career was odd from the start. I didn't begin dancing until I was nineteen. I'm excluding the one combination ballet–tap class I took as a little girl because I quit in order to pursue gymnastics. My love of dance still lay dormant when I entered Hunter College with plans to study accounting. Three semesters later, I left college, got hooked on Jazzercise and then jazz dance classes. I had very little knowledge of modern dance when I returned to Hunter, enrolled in Fundamentals of Modern Dance, and majored in dance.

A guidance counselor at Hunter, who was a major supporter of the dance program, approached me after class one day and asked, "What are you planning to do? Dance administration?" Hunter's program prepared students of all shapes and sizes for careers in teaching, performing, and administration. From her perspective, I was not a performer, but auditions were not required to declare a dance major, so my path seemed free of obstacles.

Without hesitation, I smiled at her and replied, "No, I'm going to perform."

My years as a gymnast helped with flexibility and determination and gave me a love of movement, but I was oblivious to the craft of dance. In two and a half years, Hunter's program helped me to discover the true essence of classic modern dance. Movement comes from who you are inside. Physicality doesn't limit an artist. Even though I wasn't the most experienced dancer in the Hunter College Dance Company, Jim chose me for the "Time to Laugh" solo. His confidence told me that dedication leads to desired and expected outcomes. Shortly before I graduated, the guidance counselor called me to her office to say, "I really have to apologize for not believing you had the ability to perform. You're ready."

After we completed *Time* at Hunter, Jim became ill. I never saw him again, even though he lived in my neighborhood. We spoke on the phone about his health and my continuing studies at the Limón studio. Jim would tell me about Limón dancers visiting him. "They say you're dancing beautifully." I knew Jim wasn't likely to recover, but I hoped he would. I hoped to see him in class at the Limón studio and to dance with him in the company one day.

Jim died four months after I graduated. It was inconceivable to me that such a generous, gifted human being could die at the age of thirty-one. As part of Jim's memorial at Hunter, I joined hands with my old classmates and members of the Limón Company to dance *Time*'s opening circle. I vowed to pass on the lessons Jim taught me. Every time I stepped through the Limón studio doors, I imagined him looking over me.

After performing with Limón on the *Missa Brevis* tour, I auditioned for an open spot in the company. It was the first opening in two years. After the final day of the audition, as I waited for the elevator, I peered through the small, square windows into the empty dance space. I first came here when Jim sent me to learn "Laugh." At the time, I was petrified to work with a Limón soloist outside of Hunter. Since then, I'd started and ended so many days here in class. I was scheduled to teach beginner technique classes in this very room. The elevator bell dinged, and I got a terrible sense that my life as a Limón dancer was over. I knew, in my heart, the director was going to choose a well-seasoned performer, also from the *Missa Brevis* tour.

I said goodbye to the studio and Jim. His lessons no longer seemed to apply to my life. The Limón technique spoke to me physically and spiritually, but if I wasn't wanted, I couldn't go back. What about the teaching gig? The announcement had already appeared in the dance section of the newspaper. I'd placed a clipping in my dance scrapbook along with the many *Missa Brevis* programs. If I wasn't good enough for the company, I couldn't teach classes like some pathetic wannabe. I removed the newspaper announcement from my scrapbook and tore it into tiny pieces.

Don't limit yourself. Why did I ever believe Limón was my destiny? I suppose I'd listened to the voices I wanted to hear. When I studied with Ruth Currier, a former Limón principal dancer, and I told her I'd started dancing at nineteen years old, she said, "You are one of *those* people who were just born to dance."

What about the company member who took me aside backstage during the *Missa Brevis* tour? *There Is a Time* was on the program that night. She told me, "I was thinking of you during the 'Closing Circle,' and your performance of 'Laugh.' It's going to happen." It meant everything to me that she could visualize my acceptance into the company.

When the rejection call came, I looked up to God. "Why?" Then, relying on my good old I-can-live-through-anything strategy, I said, "Okay, if not this, then what?"

When I was a little girl, I would sit with my father in his brown recliner. He would sing a silly Italian nursery rhyme that ended in a tickle session. His voice was deep and gravelly from years of smoking. He wore thick, black-rimmed glasses and sported a thin comb-over. He walked with a limp, ate pot pie and pickled pigs' feet. He was a longshoreman, a regular usher at ten o'clock mass, and he never cursed. That and less than a handful of moments is all I remember about my father.

I always wanted children, and like many women, my age played a major part of the numbers game. I wanted at least two by the time I was thirty-five. I placed this limit on myself because my father died at the age of fifty-three, and I wanted to be alive long enough to see my children into adulthood. I wanted them to remember me.

I didn't dream about my children winning the Nobel Peace Prize or hitting home runs in the World Series. I hoped to give them the type of childhood that would make them sit around the Christmas table hungry for old stories and a glimpse of photo albums. I enjoyed watching and listening as John's siblings reminisced:

"Do you remember when we lived in the projects, and Mom spray-painted those gold dots on the walls?"

"Do you remember how she used all our beds as pasta drying racks?"

"Do you remember the jeweled Easter eggs she made?"

"She made the best apple pie. And corn muffins. And cinnamon rolls. What about the Friday night pizza? I loved eating the leftovers cold on Saturday morning."

I hoped my children would take after my mother, who had gotten up and thrown me a birthday party two weeks after her husband died, and every year on the anniversary of his death, she would call my brother and his wife to wish them many more years of happiness together.

The thrill of my first pregnancy ended during my first sonogram. Dr. Mayer couldn't find a heartbeat. Trying to give me and John hope, he said, "Perhaps at just six weeks, it's too early to see it. Come back next week." With cramping and minor back pain, I had already suspected a problem. Years of dance training taught me how to listen to every fiber of my physical being, and I trusted that mind–body relationship. The following week, we were sitting with Dr. Mayer staring at a sonogram picture of an empty, collapsing sac.

I was not the first woman in my family to experience a miscarriage. I had grown up with matter-of-fact stories of my aunts' and mother's losses. Unlike mine, their misses were dramatic scenes of heavy bleeding and rushing to hospitals. My body didn't seem to want to let go of the pregnancy. After a surgical "cleaning out," I silently wondered why this was the start to my motherhood story. As far as I knew, none of my relatives had lost their first child.

I read that most women don't share their miscarriage experiences. I told very few people, but those that I did tell assured me the next baby would be fine. I bought into the idea that my loss would be replaced by the family I was meant to have. To ensure a better second pregnancy, I gave my body more than the recommended time to heal, read detailed books on conception, and even insisted my doctor perform a uterine biopsy to be sure there was nothing physically wrong with me.

When I was a child, I walked around rubbing a pillow stuffed under my shirt, dreaming about how sensational pregnancy would feel. This might very well have been the first unrealistic dream I conjured up, but I was grounded enough not to dismiss the pain of childbirth. I don't know how old I was when I asked my mother about labor, but I was young enough to believe her when she said, "It's a loving kind of pain." My childhood fantasies didn't prepare me for the all-day "morning sickness" that lingered for four months into my pregnancy with Benjamin.

Month by month, I began to question the amount of pain I would be able to endure. Just when I thought I couldn't get through another minute of nausea, I saw a bump push up out of my belly. I didn't know anyone who had seen movement at just seventeen weeks along. I figured it was a sign of a strong baby. I placed my hand on my stomach and thanked my unborn child for the sign of encouragement. "You keep growing. You're worth all my suffering."

In the first months of Benjamin's life, when our worries were growing, I'd reach out to my mom. She was the insightful yet give-it-to-you-straight kind of mom whom every kid on the block turned to. Questions about peer pressure and drugs? Discussing birth control? No problem. She'd been raising kids since she was nineteen, and there wasn't a child-rearing question she couldn't answer, from constipation to measles. Even the women I babysat for in my teens would call "Dr. Nana" before going to their pediatricians. Now when we spoke on the phone, I could hear her holding back tears. "Jo, I don't know why God is doing this to you. I wish it wasn't true, but I love you and John and Benjamin." Nothing was right with my world, and no amount of faith and prayers could stand up to the fact that motherhood, like dance, was a dream created to die.

How many times could I redefine my purpose? Finding the strength to leave dance and believing my Limón failure was a sign to move on had felt right at the time, but I'd chastised myself for ignoring Jim's warning and lamented over the fact that my bigger failure was wasting all that Jim and dance had taught me. It took two years for me to figure out what to do with my life.

In the summer of 1993, John and I married, and I went back to Hunter College to work on my master's in special education. To this day, people look perplexed when I tell them I was a dancer before going into special education, as if one career had nothing to do with the other, but I had come to believe performing prepared me for standing up in front of a classroom. Plus, special education seemed a natural path to take after teaching dance and gymnastics over the years to so many children with attention-deficit/hyperactivity disorder, autism, and minor physical disabilities. Recently, John confessed his early confusion about my decision to leave dance. "It was like you were in Triple-A baseball about to get called up, and you quit. I couldn't understand why you were so certain about walking away."

Seeing it from his point of view made me realize how little I appreciated all that I had accomplished as a professional dancer. For a short time, I did try to continue performing as a guest at Hunter and with smaller companies, but I couldn't replace the love I had for Limón until I discovered my passion for special education. I had no idea I was building a critical personal foundation.

While most other parents were busy watching their five-month-old babies roll over, play with toys, and babble, John and I were having Benjamin's head painstakingly wired for his second EEG. Sometimes medicine is so old-fashioned and bar-baric. The test started with more head measurements and red pencil markings on his scalp. Red, the color used to mark mistakes in school. Red marks all over my child's head. I never liked making mistakes, and by high school, that attribute had become my trademark. In my yearbook, my psychology teacher wrote, "Someday soon, realize how very good you are and the impossibility of knowing everything. Relax in the joy of learning. God keep you in His care." Life is not that simple. I perseverate over my failures, like a script the nuns forced me to write. *I will not chew gum in school. I will not chew gum in school.*

Over and over, as Benjamin lay on the table, the technician placed more than twenty electrodes on his skull, applied glue, and dried them with a blow of air. The smell of the glue didn't seem fit for infant exposure. The loud air compressor made Benjamin cry. With John once again sequestered to the waiting room, I sang alone.

"Momma loves Ben," I whispered, kissing his cheek.

My stoic demeanor was nothing but a lie. I hoped he couldn't sense the truth. The sight of my baby in a wire turban disturbed me. Did he feel I had betrayed him? I had given him this life.

The technician turned off the lights, and Benjamin calmed down. When she flashed the strobe lights at him, he closed his eyes and pushed his head back. *There's our Dracula.* Benjamin fell asleep, exhausted from the struggle of the test prep. A month earlier, during his first EEG, we had sedated him with chloral hydrate. I was relieved to avoid the medication this time and more grateful Benjamin wouldn't remember any of it. When the test was finished, the tech used another offensive chemical to detach each electrode. We had arrived with Benjamin covered in the sweet smell of baby products and left with a damp lab rat. I couldn't wait to get him home and wash the clinical odor off his head.

The next milestone to achieve was the dreaded MRI. The CAT scan wasn't sufficient after all. With no hope for a positive outcome, it was an exercise of mental stability. John, tired of waiting rooms, decided not to miss another day of work.

Fortunately, this sedation experience was smoother than the first, and no one escorted me out of the room. This time I held my prayers. With nothing to occupy my mind, I focused on the MRI tunnel. The machine was loud, clicking and beeping. I watched the digital numbers count down the time for each picture to be finished. It was cold in the room, but I didn't care. I was dead inside, but goosebumps and raised hair were signs of life, so that felt good. I couldn't figure out why, but obviously, this pain was mine. Whatever I had done in my last life to deserve this, I hoped it was worth it. Benjamin slept all the way home and for hours after that. I waited for him to wake and eat. I waited for results. I cried and I waited.

Even though John and I were incredibly sad, we tried hard to enjoy parenthood. We still played typical, silly infant games with Benjamin, read to him, and engaged him. We loved this little boy, and nothing would ever change that. We gave him a host of endearing nicknames: BenjaboyD, Benjabeany, Benjabeauty. We made up songs. His favorite was set to the tune of "Shortnin' Bread." "Who loves the Benjamin, Benjamin, Benjamin? Who loves the Benjamin, Benjamin boy? Mama loves the Benjamin, Benjamin, Benjamin. Mama loves the Benjamin, Benjamin boy." We sang multiple verses by replacing "Mama" with Daddy, Grandma, and every aunt and uncle.

It was only our family and inner circle of friends who knew exactly what was happening. Outside our dining room window, the backyard reflected a chaotic truth. Weeds had overrun the grass. Four feet in height, they were a visual daily symbol of how out of control life had been for the past six months. It would have been easy to cut the grass early on, but we just couldn't do it. Now we didn't even have the necessary equipment to get the job done. I imagined our neighbors thought we were just too joyously busy with a newborn to attend to the yard. I stared at the growing jungle and wondered whether we would gain control of anything ever again.

As I cried every day at his crib side, Benjamin would laugh at me. Inevitably, I would be able to smile back at him because that is just one of his many gifts. When people see Benjamin in the street, they don't look at him with fear or sadness. They smile at him. You would have to meet him to understand how he is capable of bringing such joy. It is just who he is.

Our family and friends adored Benjamin. They saw in him what we did. His eyes reflected a pure and simple brilliance. It was a painful kind of love. I didn't know how to stop the deep, desperate, dark, ugly, helpless feelings. I fired every one of Benjamin's dead grandparents—my father, stepfather, and both of John's parents were useless guardian angels. I threatened God. *I'll never teach again. I'll never help another child if you do this to him.* I didn't mean it. I knew it was one of the stages of grief. I started teaching gymnastics when I was fourteen years old. Working with children was a passion that grew stronger over the three years I taught preschool special education.

Before I ever heard the word *lissencephaly,* I brought Benjamin to meet my coworkers. It's eerie to think of the numerous special educators and therapists who held him that day. None of us knew Benjamin's disabilities would exceed those of all of the children in the building. He stared into everyone's eyes, giving them his undivided attention. One of the therapists made a point to say, "It's so nice to hold a normal, responsive baby."

When I was pregnant, I shared what I had hoped were paranoid concerns. "It feels like the baby is shaking. Is it normal to see the baby's kicks at only seventeen weeks?"

My fellow teachers would reassure me, "The special needs

population is small. You only think it's common because you see these kids every day."

What more could I do but agree? "Of course, I'll deal with whatever God gives me." But with a degree in learning disabilities, I was most comfortable instructing the students with mild/ moderate disabilities. I'd look at the students with severe disabilities, thinking, *I wouldn't even know how to teach them.* The kids were well-behaved and enjoyed school. I just didn't know how the teacher filled the time with such a slow pace and endless repetition.

Now, teaching anyone was out of the question. I had no option but to give up my career. Benjamin's needs were growing, and I was the primary caregiver. While it's true that John squeezed in as much time as possible holding, kissing, and photographing Benjamin on weekends, his work in the film industry often had him out of the house before the sun was up and home past my bedtime. He'd meet me at doctor appointments whenever possible and then disappear. I don't know how he was able to digest the information and function for so many hours at work, but keeping a roof over our heads and providing medical insurance were his burden. Or maybe his escape.

Meanwhile, my love-filled heart was breaking down into a million pieces. I suppose everyone has had a loss that brings that kind of pain, but being heartbroken over your child is different. A mother is supposed to be able to fix the boo-boos, not cause them. There was no logical reason for me to feel guilty. I knew this. I didn't purposefully hurt Benjamin. I followed prenatal care to the letter. I was in great shape before the pregnancy, at optimal weight. I never ate healthier. I did everything "right," and still everything turned out completely wrong for him.

I had failed Benjamin. He was broken beyond anyone's ability to fix him. My thirty-two-year-old, ex-dancer body had failed another baby. Would my dreams always end up as failures? Would my heart ever be able to separate Benjamin from his disabilities?

Dr. Gold continued to be direct yet caring when delivering the EEG and MRI results. Abnormal. The EEG was abnormal. That gave us a whole new set of worries. The results suggested the presence of a seizure disorder. That lingering startle reflex was becoming more and more troublesome. He suggested we start Benjamin on phenobarbital.

After consulting with my friend Ann, the school psychologist, we decided to hold off on the medication until we could do an inpatient twenty-four-hour video EEG to confirm actual seizures. Unfortunately, our insurance wouldn't cover the test at that point. It didn't make any sense. Didn't they understand the implications of giving an infant such a powerful drug? Ann said phenobarbital reduces IQ. Benjamin had enough problems. We were just beginning to build his unknown cognitive functioning and didn't want to negatively affect his IQ with serious medications without certain clinical proof he needed it.

My family started ranting about all the drug addicts in the world who had perfectly healthy babies. So that's where I went wrong. I should have been a drug addict. Perhaps if I hadn't taken such good care of my body, Benjamin wouldn't have survived the pregnancy, and he wouldn't be suffering. Good to imagine, by the way, that even a drug addict can do the one thing I had wanted to do all my life but couldn't: have a normal, healthy child. It was ridiculous for me to make such judgmental comparisons, but I suppose that's what people under extreme stress do.

Then came the MRI results: "Markedly abnormal with evidence of diffuse cerebral atrophy and lissencephaly. . . ." There was that mystery diagnosis again, *lissencephaly*. John and I searched every neurology textbook at the hospital's medical bookstore. The most we could find was one small paragraph on this rare brain malformation. Frustrated by the lack of information, we contacted a friend who worked in computer programming. She was only able to find one matching result on the Internet, a lissencephaly support group. Their motto was "Touched Briefly for All Eternity." A greater sense of doom and dread was born within me. This way of thinking was so contrary to how I functioned as a teacher. I would never place a limit on my expectations for my students. Like Jim, I would never encourage my students to limit themselves. My job was to guide them toward their undefined potential. The meaning behind that motto held my original version of motherhood hostage. It created a hierarchy of conflict I wasn't sure I could climb.

I flipped through Benjamin's photo album, already filled with more photos than I possessed of my own childhood. The first pages displayed sonogram pictures and one of John standing behind me pulling my shirt tight to show my ever-so-slight baby bump. There were baby shower photos and close-ups of my huge belly with a tiny pair of booties hanging on our Christmas tree in the background, and even one picture of me bored and on bed rest in the last month due to high blood pressure.

Of course, the day of Benjamin's induced birth produced many photos of our seven-pound, fourteen-ounce bundle. The next pages showed Benjamin sleeping, nursing, bathing, and lounging in front of the windows for sun exposure to keep his bilirubin numbers down. We captured story time, diaper changes, and Benjamin's amazing eye gaze. We staged him sitting up on our bed with the remote control and telephone and lying down using our cat as a pillow. Benjamin sported numerous gifted outfits throughout. Page after page, his thighs got fatter, his smile wider, and his eyes brighter.

Any unsuspecting person would think it all looked so happy and normal. I ran my hand along the page of overlapping baptism pictures, displayed like a strip of film showing the moment we stood on the altar as the priest poured the holy water over Benjamin's head. My brother James and John's sister were Benjamin's godparents. They arrived early that morning to dress him in his little white suit and delicate gold crucifix. We walked to the church, accepting well-wishes from neighbors and strangers.

Even though I felt a sense of dread when I compared Benjamin to the other babies, and I couldn't quite get his head upright when we took pictures with the priest, we made promises to God and the church. Promises I wasn't sure how to keep in the face of the pictures of Benjamin as I saw them now. His head was so obviously small, his legs stiff and straight, his arms held tightly up against his torso with his fists resting under his chin. My body ached for him to have freedom of movement. Why did I ever think God made promises to me?

I placed the album back in my closet, on the bookshelf next to the medical binder that held Benjamin's test results, next to the scrapbook filled with newspaper clippings and programs from old dance concerts.

3

Drop the Weight

A time to kill, and a time to heal

Modern dancers use various types of movements and dynamics in order to tell a story or evoke an emotion. They manipulate their use of weight, space, and time to create movement that's fast or slow, fluid or sharp. I understood space and time—go from here to there in eight counts—but weight was a trickier concept. Releasing your weight into the movement makes everything much easier, stressless, but it's so common to hold back.

Jim used a simple lesson to teach that in order to learn how to use weight to your advantage, you must first acknowledge the weight you have. Tall and lean, he'd stand in the front of the studio, facing us as he demonstrated. "Stand on two feet. Now take hold of one leg with both hands under the knee. Allow it to hang limply. Lift the leg up and down a bit. Hmmm. Ask yourself, how heavy is this leg? What would happen if I dropped it?" I can hear the collective thump of an entire class of dancers dropping their legs and allowing their feet to land hard on the wooden floor. The room shook.

Fall *and* Recovery

❧

When Benjamin was born in 1999, my life as a dancer was eight years behind me, except for a few guest appearances at Hunter. My last performance before motherhood had been just three short years before Benjamin was born. It seemed more like a hundred years, or someone else's life. Not mine. My time at Hunter was irrelevant compared to my son's assumed shortened life-span.

John and I bought a computer so I could join the online lissencephaly support group. John, who was always a fiercely private person, wasn't interested in exposing himself to a bunch of strangers. I respected his need to find his own way to balance our reality, even if I couldn't subscribe to his solitary process.

I realized early in our marriage that our parents had raised us to manage conflict and grief differently. John's family seemed to avoid confrontation. When they fought, they didn't speak to each other, sometimes for months. My family was direct and loud, analyzing the hell out of a situation. We slammed doors and punched walls, but no one went to bed angry.

John and I didn't sit around discussing our feelings. He was generally quiet when I shared information from the lissencephaly families. I took that as a sign of our mutual pain and found comfort in the idea that John's heart was as heavy as mine, but as wonderful as John was as a husband and father, I felt alone. My experience felt unique because I was the mommy. No amount of conversation was going to relieve my sense of isolation. John couldn't resolve my feelings of guilt and inadequacy for me. I had to find a way to release that weight on my own.

The truth is, we were both in crisis. The old saying is: Hardships either bring you together or pull you apart. I suppose some people think holding on tighter helps them to find a balance, but it's not possible to have a sense of stability when you're both falling. John and I built our marriage on the secure knowledge that sometimes, in order to stay together, you have to give the other person a little extra space. In my vows I wrote, "You need not hold on so tightly to something you already have. You need only to trust in our ability to grow within ourselves and still be able to walk side by side."

The support group was my first real lifeline, and I began climbing my way back up to a sanity that seemed to have escaped me. Everyone understood the grief, the loss, the frustration, and the future. They had more to offer me than anyone else did. "Talking" with other parents in similar circumstances was comforting because they just "got it." I could ask anything and share anything. I didn't have to hold back. They had been where I was, had the same questions and anxieties, and had found some of the answers.

I sat glued to my computer, monitoring my email inbox for posts from the "Loop" members. I "listened" to their histories and tried to use them to solve the great mystery of how and why. They offered models that proved I could survive the whole journey. No doubt, the more families I "met," the more daunting that journey appeared. Lissencephaly is a rare neuronal migration disorder. When the brain forms, cells migrate from the center of the brain toward the cortex, the outermost layer. Imagine a picture of the brain with all those lovely convolutions. With lissencephaly, the cells fail to follow the proper sequence of movement. They don't quite make it from one place to the other, so the outer layer of the brain is smooth. The doctors couldn't detect it until the later part of pregnancy. In 1999, sonograms were not reliable enough for diagnosing microcephaly prenatally. Some known genetic mutations existed. At least one family tried, but failed, to prove environmental causes.

I fed off this small yet diverse group of people as if I had just arrived for dinner after imprisonment on an obscure, barren island. They taught me about medications, early intervention, health insurance, therapeutic equipment, practitioners, and the potential physical complications. I printed out their collective knowledge on every topic for future use. Doctors could make recommendations and go by their limited medical studies, but these families were on the front line. The support group gave me personal data. I placed it all in a binder, uncertain whether John would ever look at it. I couldn't force him to accept this group or to feel the sense of support and relief they gave me. I could only hope he was healing in his own way.

In the evenings, when Benjamin slept and John was at work, the house was too quiet. I would stay up late instant messaging on AOL with parents. It was often hard to sleep when every month a family would email about the death of their child. We were able to meet a few local families in person. The children varied greatly, having a spectrum of abilities as with any disorder. Most of the families had children under five. A few kids were older, and only one was near twenty.

One of the mothers on the Loop explained, "Children with lissencephaly have difficulty maintaining physical capabilities as they grow. They just don't have the brainpower." Many kids had chronic pneumonia. I kept hearing, "That's what usually gets them." Most of the children had severe seizure disorders. Unstoppable seizures sent parents rushing to the hospital as their children fought to breathe. Some kids had tracheostomies and feeding tubes. The orthopedic issues were numerous with hip dislocations and scoliosis. Information about life-span varied, but it was not uncommon to read that it was only to age two. Certainly, we could see there were exceptions to that rule. I listened to those parents, and even though they were providing a support service I couldn't live without, they scared the hell out of me.

As suggested by the doctor who compared my son's brain to a cake, I worked on securing home-based early intervention services. Since I was the special educator and now a stay-at-home mom, John handed that project over to me. Even though I had the right education and experience to get the job done, it was a heavy task. I hired, then fired the first agency I contacted, fearing I had made a hasty decision. So I called my coworkers, school district administrators, and then multiple therapeutic agencies until my gut told me: *This one. They've listened, patiently answered every question. Their interest and dedication are genuine. They know what they're doing.*

Benjamin's first case coordinator listened attentively during our first phone conversation as I detailed the ugly truths about lissencephaly. "Some of the babies die before their first birthday. What is the purpose of watching a baby suffer? There are times I wonder why he survived the pregnancy. What kind of terrible mother can even think such a thing?"

Although she would later confess that she didn't believe Benjamin was at risk of dying until her boss reviewed the lissencephaly information I faxed to them, she handled my questions without pity. She insisted, "You're a loving mother. Lots of new moms have terrible thoughts. I suffered from postpartum depression. I would look at my healthy child and wish she was gone." I was grateful to her for sharing this. She made me feel like a normal parent at a time when I had dissociated myself from that group.

We set up an "Interim Individualized Family Service Plan," an emergency plan of sorts that allowed Benjamin to receive services before a formal evaluation. It was a tremendous relief to get a break from the pressure I had placed on myself as a teacher and former dancer to devise a therapeutic curriculum. Every day I put Benjamin through a routine of infant toys, reading, classical music, and choreographed stretching exercises for his arms and legs. I was ready to hand over the lesson plan book to someone else so I could get back to just being Mommy. We started with physical and occupational therapies, and I could finally feel a foothold. I was at the beginning of my training, preparing for a lifetime of mountain climbing.

Children referred for early intervention undergo an "arena" style evaluation to determine eligibility and severity of delay. Benjamin's team included a special educator, an occupational therapist, and a human services specialist. I led the three women to a spare bedroom. Baby blankets covered the area rug, and a dining room table stood up against the wall acting as a storage unit for all of Benjamin's favorite toys. I suppose it looked like a typical playroom, but there was nothing normal about having a designated therapy space for an infant. Toys weren't playthings but a means to a therapeutic end.

I placed Benjamin in the center of a quilted red blanket and sat back to observe. The three women gathered on the floor around him. The special educator spoke gently. "Hi, Benjamin." She turned to me. "Do you call him Benjamin, or does he have a nickname? Ben, Benny?"

"He has a lot of nicknames, but you can call him Benjamin." I hated the name Benny. It reminded me of the character on the once popular TV show *L.A. Law* who had intellectual disabilities. I refused to call my baby boy Benny and imagine him as a disabled adult.

She began again, "Benjamin, we're going to play together. I'm going to pick you up." We all watched as she held him upright, then across her lap, and back to the blanket to perform the head lag test. No matter what position she placed him in, he still couldn't lift his head. She held a toy above him to look at and moved it slowly side to side. His eyes followed it back and forth. She asked me, "What's his favorite toy?"

I offered, "Show him the stuffed horsey. If you squeeze its sides, it neighs."

She galloped the horse on his belly. He smiled. "Do you want the horsey, Benjamin? Come get the horsey." He made some vocalizations and laughed, but he couldn't reach for it.

The OT noted his body position. "He still has his

asymmetrical tonic neck reflex." He looked like he was lying in a fencer's en garde position. She held his hands and stretched his arms out. After quickly releasing them, Benjamin startled. Another notation: "He still has his Moro reflex." She turned him over to his belly. I cringed. With his face flat to the quilt, he started to cry. Turning him over again, she tried to soothe him: "I'm sorry, Benjamin. Here comes the horsey."

"What else calms him down when he cries?" she asked. I handed her his pacifier. She placed it in his mouth. After only thirty minutes, he fell asleep. I couldn't blame him for shutting down. At least one of us had escaped the stress.

Now they turned the spotlight on me. "We can let him sleep, and you can give us the rest of the details we need to finish the evaluation." I had expected to feel a comfort being in my own home as opposed to being in a doctor's office. You know, it's better to be on your own turf. Now my turf, my home, had been infiltrated by the reality that we needed a team of professionals to address the needs of my infant boy.

They stripped me down with their questions.

"Any problems with the pregnancy?"

"What prenatal tests did you have?"

"Was he born full-term? Vaginally?"

"What were his measurements? Apgar? Head circumference?"

"How long were you in the hospital after giving birth?"

"Are you breastfeeding?"

"What doctors do you see?"

"How often does he eat/sleep/excrete?"

"What does he like/dislike?"

Thinking of my son's every minute behavior made my head spin. I simultaneously interpreted the purpose of their questions and reflected on Benjamin's poor performance. I sat with my back against the pale-yellow wall, looking up at the gray ceiling. It now seemed horribly appropriate that we chose this color scheme for all our bedrooms before Benjamin was born. I wished away the tears as they fell. *Why did we have to need all of this?*

Once the team wrote up their reports, I received an invitation to my first complete Individualized Family Service Plan meeting to update the interim plan already in place. The agency's office occupied space in a typical Brooklyn brownstone. We gathered in a living room, overcrowded with furniture and office paraphernalia. I had plenty of experience meeting with school district administrators to fight for services on behalf of my preschool students, but this was the first time I had attended a full-fledged meeting sitting on the parents' side of the table.

As we reviewed Benjamin's results, I thought of the parents I had worked with in the past and realized I could have done a better job managing the parents' needs. New teachers have so much energy, enthusiasm, and current research. You could say I fit into that category prior to Benjamin's birth. I was a very confident educator, but now I was beginning to see I hadn't understood the parents at all. To be fair, I didn't see the parents on a regular basis. The students were all bused to school, but still I knew I'd made certain judgments about the parents' behavior. If a parent refused to respond to my notes or requests, I assumed they didn't care enough or weren't capable of taking an active role in their child's education. I couldn't feel the full force of their responsibilities, challenges, or emotions. Now I was on the journey to discovering the truth about what it means to have a child with a disability. The comfy couch I was sitting on did little to cushion my heavy heart and bruised ego.

In addition to occupational and physical therapies, Benjamin qualified for special instruction and also speech therapy, which was a surprise to me. What would a speech therapist do with a six-month-old? The one course I had in college covering early intervention wasn't enough to understand the entire system of care. It turns out that speech therapists can work on feeding issues and focus on oral motor functioning, which of course plays a very big part in being able to speak. I was alarmed at all the support services that Benjamin had qualified for in general. Grateful but stunned. It was a sign of just how developmentally delayed he already was.

The team also offered counseling services for me on a weekly basis. I felt like they were handing me the right tools to help our whole family cope. I felt fortunate because, even though I was at a complete loss at the start of the process, all I had to do was pick up the phone and call my trusted coworkers to put me on track.

Time is crucial at the start. By the time you surrender to reality and reach out for services, you already feel like you're running late to help your child. How do parents without my resources and a degree in special education navigate the system and their feelings at the same time? It was refreshing to be able to think beyond myself again for the moment. It was the start of a transformation, I suppose.

Unfortunately, change doesn't always signify progress. Benjamin's once-isolated Moro reflex morphed into a collection of startles. As a shock approached, his eyes would widen until his limbs would shoot outward. Right after the jolt, his eyes would roll upward. As his body relaxed, his eyes would shut, and he'd cry until the building wave would silence him and widen his eyes again. In five minutes, there were twenty or thirty clusters of movement, some slow to build, others rapid-fire. I rode the unpredictable ebb and flow as it moved through his body. My muscles tensed at the sight of my baby's brain conducting an electrocution. I had no power to ease his suffering.

Knowing our concerns regarding phenobarbital, the neurologist suggested another medication, Klonopin, which eliminated the startles but left Benjamin lethargic. He lost his sucking reflex. My breasts were engorged from a lack of nursing. I called Dr. Gabriel. "Benjamin's not eating. He can't even suck his pacifier."

He sighed, "You can't let him dehydrate. It happens quicker than you think. Pump and use an eyedropper to feed him. Give him a little bit every few minutes." Not one of the hospital parenting classes John and I took had prepared me for this. Dr. Gold reduced the dosage of Klonopin, but then the seizures returned.

With the first failed medication experiment completed, our insurance would now cover the inpatient video EEG. Once we knew what type of seizure Benjamin was dealing with, the neurologist could determine the appropriate medication instead of just throwing drugs at us. A twenty-four-hour continuous study produced a visual drawing of Benjamin's brain waves. Unlike the comforting patterns of print in a book or symbols on sheets of music, the lines played a loud and chaotic rhythm representing a special type of seizure disorder called infantile spasms.

It was yet another devastating diagnosis. Infantile spasms are a rare and extremely difficult-to-manage form of epilepsy. It was paramount to get them under control before they eliminated any hope for developmental progress. Each series of seizures felt like the burning down of a bridge we would never get access to again. When I looked into Benjamin's eyes, he seemed farther and farther away. He smiled less often.

The neurology team gave John and me a list of medication options, complete with success rates and potential life-threatening side effects. To save our seven-and-a-half-month-old from seizing to death, we would have to fill him with drugs. Harmful drugs. All my diligent prenatal care seemed wasted. To think that I scrutinized the use of acetaminophen during my pregnancy. It was trivial compared to weighing one death sentence against another.

One year of college biology did not nearly qualify me to play doctor or even first-year medical student, but when it came to lissencephaly and infantile spasms, the doctors didn't have all the answers. They would guide us, but John and I had the final say. We were now part of the new reality of doctor–parent relationships. In regard to Benjamin's care, we would be the experts, no one else. As a special educator, I'd tell parents, "You know your child better than any collection of specialists," but that concept did little for me now. How could we make the right decision? Benjamin would suffer the consequences of any false move we made.

My mood was as toxic as the choices given. Thanks to the hospital's only-one-parent-overnight rule, I spent the night of the EEG without John, watching Benjamin suffer roughly two hundred seizures. For every jolt, I pressed a button on the computer attached to all the wires on his head. I recorded my observations on a chart, neatly at first. "Upper and lower extremity extensions. Eye roll. Crying." By mid-page I was using abbreviations, "UE, LE." My notes were entirely illegible by the bottom of the page.

A newborn occupied the other half of the room. In the morning, a team of doctors huddled around her crib. "Excuse us," one of them said to me, drawing the dividing curtain. "We have the results of your daughter's blood work," I heard him say through the thin fabric. "Her seizures are due to a calcium imbalance. We can treat her very easily."

"Thank you so much. You'll give her the supplement? We can go home?" the mother said. I was happy for her, but the bunkmate bond we had established was gone. I would never feel such relief. Had I completely lost my sense of humanity?

John and I had an impossible decision to make. Breaking his typical silent way of dealing with things, John admitted, "Benjamin might not make it to his first birthday." Like the divorce comment, his willingness to vocalize his pessimistic view frightened me. But this time, he'd hit on a fear we were both entertaining. We decided that the only way to make this type of choice was to think about our future selves. Years from now, we wanted to be able to get out of bed and look in the mirror with the least possible amount of guilt.

John and I reviewed the list of medications, grilled the

epilepsy team, and agreed that our goal for Benjamin was to reap the most benefit with the least amount of physical risk. We decided to start Benjamin on Vigabatrin, a front-line treatment for infantile spasms. Its most concerning potential side effect was a permanent loss of peripheral vision. We figured that was something Benjamin could live without. Although we agreed on its safety, it was not FDA approved and therefore not covered by insurance. We would have to buy it from a pharmacy in Canada.

We cared about Benjamin more than our financial ruin. After an unsuccessful three-week trial, the seizures forced us to return to the hospital for the next antiseizure drug on the list. ACTH, a short-term treatment with the potential for long-term results, had to be secured through a special program with the National Organization for Rare Diseases. We trained to accurately measure and administer the medication via intramuscular injections. Our days consisted of little glass medicine bottles, syringes, needles, and sacrificial oranges that we practiced on.

Growing more desperate to stop the seizures, we swung from one extreme to the other. ACTH's list of potential side effects was staggering and included an increase in appetite, weight gain, acne, increased glucose, high blood pressure, cardiac problems, gastrointestinal bleeding, and irritability. It was a strange thing to focus on, but I hated most that a medication had the potential to alter Benjamin's mood. Even if we did manage to stop the seizures, I couldn't imagine surviving one day without seeing Benjamin's smile or hearing his laughter. I was afraid that if he lost his brilliant disposition, his love-filled eyes would only reflect misery. Of course, the seizures were already doing all of that.

We prepared to monitor Benjamin closely. Even though a visiting nurse would check his vitals two or three times a week, it was our responsibility to place test strips in his diaper to monitor his sugar and smear a sample of stool in another test kit to check for blood. I learned to manually check his blood pressure.

Realizing that, with a nonverbal child, diagnosing any illness would depend on a process of elimination, I bought an otoscope to keep a lookout for ear infections. After our hospital training was finished, and he'd had a thorough baseline cardiac workup, we went home, even though there was no immediate improvement in Benjamin's seizure activity.

Injecting Benjamin twice a day was a major challenge for me. Stabbing oranges was a lot easier than piercing my son's flesh. My hand moved to and fro, aiming at Benjamin as if he were a dartboard. I'm not sure if it was my grip, a lack of force, or the fact that I didn't want to administer the shot, but I bounced quite a few needles off my poor baby's legs. John handled it well. He'd given his mother plenty of vitamin B-12 shots, but because of his work schedule, he could only give the weekend injections.

When I mentioned my anxiety to a neighbor, her husband, an anesthesiologist, offered to give Benjamin the shots, but I refused his help. Thickheaded and stubborn, I'm not the type to take the easy way out of anything, and the idea of giving up this responsibility made me feel like a failure. I had to find a new coping strategy. The old, I-can-survive-anything mantra no longer worked for me. Twice a day, I would draw the medication into the syringe and talk myself into the act.

You can do this.

No, I can't.

You have no choice!

It's not right. It's not fair.

Fair is a four-letter word. You think your mother's life as a forty-six-year-old widow was fair? Didn't she teach you anything about strength?

Yes, she did. My mother was born the year our country fell into the Great Depression. She was three years old when her own mother died, and she ended up with the living version of the fairy-tale stepmother who locked her in closets and refused to feed her. My mother wasn't one to sit whimpering in the dark. She banged on those doors, and when her stepmother forced her to clear the other family members' dinner plates, she licked them clean. When my father protested against her desire to work, she fought back. After my father died, she blossomed into the strong, independent woman my father didn't want her to be.

You are your mother's daughter, and you will do this for your son.

I stood over Benjamin, pinching his chunky baby flesh in one hand and the needle in the other. As I took aim, an invisible bubble encased me, robbing me of oxygen. Once I pierced his skin, I could breathe again. The serum was a thick gel, and pushing it in was painful for Benjamin. Looking at his needle-tracked thighs, I wondered if the scars would ever fade.

I sent emails to the Loop. Day or night, there was always someone in some part of the world ready to reply.

"We started Benjamin on ACTH. There's no improvement yet. For those who've been through it, how long does it take to see results? I hate giving him these shots, especially if it's not helping."

"It is hard, but don't give up. It took three weeks for us to see results. Give BenjaboyD a hug, and one for you too."

After what seemed like forever but was around two weeks, we saw the reduction of his seizures and eventually their complete elimination. Benjamin became more vibrant again and, thankfully, had few side effects. He was a hungry, bloated baby with acne, but I had no problem with that. ACTH was one of many lifesaving poisons we had come to embrace.

It was time to create an even greater sense of control. Outside our dining room window, I watched as two machete-wielding landscapers slashed through the chaotic wall of weeds and stuffed the debris into heavy-duty garbage bags. I could hear the thud of each bag landing in the dump truck. Clearing the garden was immediately satisfying. Light existed where it hadn't before. There was air to breathe and so much hope and anticipation for new growth.

4

Don't Try to Change Anything

A time to rend, and a time to sew

Jim would sometimes start class instructing us to lie on our backs and close our eyes. I'd take a deep breath and follow Jim's sporadic instructions as he wandered the studio. He was so light on his feet that I was never sure which direction his voice would come from, but I trusted he'd say the right thing. "Where are you actually making contact with the floor? What differences are there between the left and right sides of your body? Just notice. Don't try to change anything." If you had walked in, you would have seen a bunch of dancers flat on the floor doing absolutely nothing. And we were, but it was the most challenging nothingness I'd ever encountered.

Where am I making contact? My head is leaning a little to the right. Don't move it to midline. I feel the connection to the floor in both shoulders, but there's more weight on my right scapula. Well, your head is leaning that way. My shoulders are rotating outward. My palms are up. My elbows aren't making contact in the same place. Bodies are symmetrical, but not identical. It feels like more of the fingers on my left hand are touching the floor than my right. Am I holding tension in my right shoulder, or in my forearm? My fingers are relaxed. Don't move. Why are they twitching? My lower back is hyperextended, too many backbends in my lifetime. Don't shift your pelvis. Just notice. The space under my back feels as deep as the Grand Canyon. I'll check that out later. You can't drop your weight if you're tilting your pelvis. My legs are rotating outward. My calves and heels are connecting at different points. My left hip feels more open, so my left foot is making more contact.

Class would move on to standing exercises, movement phrases across the floor, and then combinations. Jim used these classes to teach the Limón technique and the *Time* choreography we'd use later in the repertory class. We were also required to complete weekly "labs" to go over anything we felt needed work. Some days I'd go over difficult movement passages, and sometimes I'd just lie on the floor, amazed at how different my body could feel from one day to the next. The funny thing is, whenever I placed a hand under that ever-annoying space under my back, it was never as big as I perceived.

My time at Hunter taught me how to challenge my perception of the world on and offstage. Once, after watching a student-choreographed piece, Jim asked us to consider the significance of one particular dancer. She'd stood in one place holding an invisible box. While the other dancers sped around the stage, interacting with each other, she held her focus on the package. Maintaining what seemed to be a precise twelve-inch space between her hands, she took almost the entire length of the dance to lower it to the ground. Compared to the other dancers, her movements were pedestrian, but it was hard to ignore her. I learned that sometimes, less is more. Silence is loud. Just notice. Different doesn't mean wrong. Different is there to challenge your perception. Life isn't always about fixing things; it's about working with what you have. Acceptance. Onstage, every movement or lack thereof has a purpose. Life isn't always so obvious with its design.

I spent my entire childhood living in a rent-controlled apartment in Brooklyn Heights. When I was twenty-three years old, my mother remarried and moved out. I was the first of my siblings to live alone. A year later, when John moved in, I was the first to live out of wedlock. The year before Benjamin was born, John and I moved out of the only home I'd ever known. I was ready to leave the place where my father died and my first pregnancy ended in miscarriage. While we could have bought a small two-bedroom apartment close by, I wanted more room to grow and outdoor space.

The moment John and I walked into a Victorian limestone in Bay Ridge, Brooklyn, I fell for the untouched original woodwork, unique center stair design, and a backyard large enough for a simple garden and a swing set. We conceived Benjamin during the first week in our new home. Toward the end of my pregnancy, our families insisted we pick a theme for the nursery. John kept saying, "Why do we need a theme? Having a baby is the theme. Why plaster a fictional character all over the room?" I agreed with him, but you can't really argue with a proud grandma and eager aunts and uncles.

Bedridden and longing to satisfy my nesting instincts, I was determined to come up with a theme we could live with. I happened to be reading *The Tao of Pooh* by Benjamin Hoff. So we chose Winnie the Pooh, the wonderfully simpleminded bear. We didn't know we were having a boy, and we didn't name our son after the author. We had made a short list of names we liked and chose Benjamin because it seemed to suit him best, and the *B* was a loving nod to John's deceased mother, Betty.

Is it a coincidence that Benjamin was destined to be as simpleminded as they come? People often tell me, "God knew what he was doing when he steered you from dance to special education. Benjamin knew what he was doing when he chose you." However you like to think about it, the irony doesn't escape me. As for Benjamin, caring for him is complicated, but he is simple, devoid of the typical distractions to affect his happiness.

Benjamin's early intervention services started off as a positive step forward, like my newly cleared garden, but the immediate satisfaction soon waned. Every day revolved around accommodating the arrivals of four separate therapists. The therapies were the number one priority, and there was no time for the typical activities I imagined we'd enjoy. No playdates, baby gym, or music classes. Playgrounds were not on the agenda. I really couldn't stand the sight of all the children running around doing things Dr. Gold seemed certain Benjamin would never be able to do. What was I going to talk to the other mothers about anyway?

I felt isolated in our 2400-square-foot house with an infant who would never move through the space on his own accord. I continued to immerse myself in the virtual parents' support group. Computer technology allowed me to travel around the globe. I contacted the world's leading authority on neuronal migration disorders. After reviewing our records, he disagreed with the lissencephaly diagnosis. He thought Benjamin had "bilateral diffuse polymicrogyria."

My Web friends were excited to hear that diagnosis, as it suggested a slightly better outcome, but the specialist was clear to say Benjamin's birth defect was widespread, so I didn't think the title change made a bit of difference. Don't get me wrong. It's great to have a specific diagnosis. I know many families who never get one. It can be frustrating not to have a name for your child's disability and no organized group to affiliate with, but words are just words, and Benjamin's deficits were speaking louder than any assumed positive prognosis.

The theory and practice of early intervention stems from the notion that early and intensive treatment can help a child to, in essence, rewire the brain. Healthy areas can take over or compensate for injured areas. Doctors believe an infant's brain is pliable, and we wanted to maximize Benjamin's potential. I never thought we were trying to fix him. I wasn't even hoping he'd prove the doctors wrong. I just hoped to see some kind of measurable change.

I realized that a transformation could take considerable time and effort. I spent two and a half years at Hunter conditioning my body in order to match my late-in-life inner drive to perform. I tried to channel that drive to help Benjamin take advantage of his therapeutic services. The physical therapist would place Benjamin on his side and tell him to roll over to his back. I'd look at his stiff torso, straight legs, clutched arms, bent elbows, and fisted hands up against his chest. I'd lie behind Benjamin cheering him on. "Hey, Benjamin, where's Mommy? Come see Mommy." One minute, two minutes, five minutes could go by. My body ached to move past this nothingness. He'd hyperextend his head in order to look at me. If we were lucky, he'd roll over because of the weight and momentum of his head movement, but none of his other body parts were free to move. I couldn't imagine how we were going to fit into the world outside of the computer group. Still, I'd clap my hands and cover his face with kisses. "Yeah, Benjamin!"

John would ask Benjamin, "Why did you have to be broken?" I hated hearing him say those words out loud. Even more, I hated that I'd asked the same question. *Broken* was never the first description anyone would use for Benjamin. It wouldn't be the first word to come to my mind either. I'm sure John felt the same, and yet that perception lived within us.

Even with all the proper supports, no one was making critical strides. Every week I hid my deepest anxieties when the social worker would ask, "How has your week been?"

Like every other week, long and lonely.

"Fine. Would you like a cup of tea?"

"No, thank you. How are Benjamin's therapies going?"

Still not making any progress.

"He cries during physical therapy, but Toby is wonderful with him. The OT made him a pair of hand splints to wear at night."

"How did that work out?"

Tell her how guilty you felt strapping his little wrists and fingers. Like putting handcuffs on a prisoner.

"I felt bad putting them on him at bedtime, but when I went to get him in the morning, they weren't on his hands anymore. I have no idea how he got them off. We're calling him Benjamini Houdini."

"Ha! So he's sleeping well."

Tell her. Mornings are harder. Every morning I open his door and stand frozen on the threshold, waiting for him to make one small movement, take one obvious breath before I can approach him. In that one pause, every single morning, I brace and prepare to see death. I don't even know what I'm hoping for. You can't tell her that.

"Well, we're both exhausted by the end of the day. I keep trying to imagine what our lives will look like in a year or two or ten."

"Joanne, I know I keep saying this, but life is a one-day-at-a-time event."

"I know," I said, looking out the dining room window and doubting I would ever be able to follow her advice. I was a planner, a master scheduler, and in order to feel as though I had any purpose, I liked to think ahead, sometimes far ahead. That habit would have to go. I might not have had specific dreams about my children, but I assumed they would have a future. How do you have a baby and fight the urge to have any aspirations for that child? How do you keep the slate clean?

Benjamin's future was empty, like the backyard. I didn't bother to plant any new seeds. I didn't have the time or energy to take care of grass or flowers. What had once seemed like a fresh start was now nothing but a big, gaping space. What is the difference between acceptance and giving up?

John and I began revealing our situation beyond our

immediate circle of friends. It was not an easy process. I couldn't call a conference with everyone we ever knew to deliver this kind of news. For the first time in my married life, I wished we were like everyone else. When John and I decided to marry, we balked tradition. John didn't get down on one knee with a box in hand. He never even proposed. We made the decision together, like the rest of our wedding plans.

Instead of a big, Brooklyn, Italian catering hall affair, we chose a gracious Georgian-style estate in Tarrytown, New York. We told our mothers, "We're paying for the wedding and keeping it small. Don't give us a list of must-invites filled with family we don't know and haven't seen since the last wedding or funeral." In the eight months it took to plan our wedding day, I fielded our family's worried comments.

"You're hiring a jazz band instead of a DJ? How is everyone supposed to dance?"

"It's jazz music. They'll dance or enjoy listening. The band performs onstage with my Hunter College professor's dance company."

"You're having buffet stations instead of a sit-down dinner? Don't expect the food to be good."

"We've tasted the food. It's delicious."

"You're not ordering matchbooks or favors?"

"The guests can take my homemade heart-shaped candles and the flowering plants that we're using as centerpieces."

"You bought a used dress?"

"It's an antique dress."

"What do you mean you don't want us to sing 'The Bride Cuts the Cake' song?"

"No cake song. No garter scene. No bouquet throwing. Please, John and I are adults. Trust us."

They all either gave up, decided to have faith, or learned to hide their feelings. No one complained when I had the seamstress cut my dress above the knee, or when John didn't pick his best man until the day of the ceremony. We didn't set out to challenge everyone's ideas of what was normal or acceptable; we were planning a wedding that would reflect who we were. John and I had the perfect wedding day. We had time to eat and mingle with our seventy guests in the large garden, and to play catch with our young nieces and nephews when they weren't busy at the activities table set up on the lawn. Afterward, we hung out with friends and family who spent the weekend with us onsite. To this day, our families admit our wedding was the best one they'd ever attended because it was so different.

When Benjamin was born, we didn't send out birth announcements, and our Christmas cards would never include a gushy family story. This kind of difference made everything seem wrong. It was a long haul, telling friends individually that yes, we had finally welcomed a beautiful baby boy into our lives but . . . I lined up unsuspecting friends in my mind as if it were a virtual funeral procession. I wrote letters to others whom I just couldn't bear to call. It was awkward, and I was tired of listening to my friends' well-wishes, their disbelief and denial. Many counted on a faith I was no longer certain I could subscribe to.

I learned a lot about people during times of crisis. Many families on the Internet support group complained about losing friends because of their child's disability. Up front, that seemed harsh and maddening. I don't know if that actually happened to us. We drifted away from some people, but I think that can be true of anyone who has children. The thought has certainly crossed my mind that some people intentionally shied away. It was disappointing to consider, but I couldn't blame anyone for that type of reaction, and certainly no one was blatantly hurtful. I didn't have it in me to be angry with anyone just because they weren't capable of handling Benjamin's disability, any more than I could blame Benjamin for putting us in this situation.

My closest friends were attentive, compassionate listeners.

Don't Try to Change Anything

My despair did not deter them from trying to coax me forward. Right after Benjamin's diagnosis, a friend of mine was home recuperating from a minor surgery. Marie called me every morning just to make sure I had gotten out of bed. It was a simple thing, but she kept me from hiding under the covers. It was important to keep moving, even if I had nowhere to go. Another friend brought Benjamin and me to the beach. As Marian drove, I spewed my saga. Her response cut right to the truth of the whole situation. "It's such a great loss." She was right, and I didn't have to see it as anything other than what it was.

I was living in a textbook situation. The parents of a child with a disability will go through the psychological equivalent of a death. The death of the child they expected to have. The death of the life they expected to lead. The only problem was that I wasn't studying for a psychology test. This was my reality.

I had to change my perception. There was nothing extraordinary about us. So what if his diagnosis was rare? We were a blip in time, less than a dot on a map, so very insignificant. I'd been pondering the wrong question. It was absurd to ask, why me? Why not me? Why did I think I was so special that I should be immune to such hardship? I didn't, but I wasn't finished mourning.

My friend Doreen told me, "I know you and John are both suffering right now. The anxiety of not knowing what lies ahead can be immobilizing. Acceptance can take years. God knows, I'm thankful for Julie every day." Doreen had been my fourth-grade teacher. After my father died, I would sit in her class reliving the moment I saw his lifeless body as I stood in my parents' doorway. Doreen would place a piece of hard candy on my desk, something sweet to clear the visions.

Throughout my high school years, we stayed in touch. I always thought we had a special bond because of my dad. Something within me knew I had to keep her in my life. There was no way to know more significant events would strengthen our attachment. Doreen's daughter has severe disabilities as well.

"Doreen, I don't think God has anything to do with it. He didn't cause Benjamin's disabilities."

"I hear you. This isn't a punishment. Benjamin is in this world for a reason. That reason will become clear to you over time. All the pain, heartache, and anxiety will teach you what is really important in life. You and John need to lean on each other. You can't have your heads in the oven at the same time. One of you has to be outside to pull the other one out."

I loved her honesty and knew mine would be welcomed. "That's great advice, Doreen, but we skipped the oven and went straight to hell. What do we do now?"

Like many of my mommy friends raising children with disabilities, Doreen advised we stock up on wine, but humor is my preferred drink. Laughter is the designated driver who steers me clear of my rubber room. Granted, parenting a child with disabilities has a way of changing the way you look at things. Nothing is simple or as you expected it to be.

Thanks to the Loop families, I had a ton of information on the few known genetic causes for neuronal migration disorders and wanted to have Benjamin tested. When I arrived at the geneticist's office, I was prepared to improve upon my education.

The geneticist walked in and asked, "Do you mind if a visiting physician observes?"

"That's fine." I understood the value of a teaching hospital, and the desire to see a rare condition up close. It doesn't always make for a comfortable situation. During one of Benjamin's hospital stays, an absurd number of doctors crowded in to take a look at his MRIs.

It was a clowns-climbing-out-of-a-tiny-car kind of thing. Or a Coney Island freak show exhibit, which is weird because I was actually wearing a Coney Island USA T-shirt on the day I gave birth to Benjamin.

The geneticist pointed toward the examination table. "Lay him down and step away." Most doctors told me to stand next to the table to make sure my eight-month-old son wouldn't fall off. I thought about protesting, but thirteen years of Catholic school had taught me to follow the rules, and I do. Plus, my Internet friends warned that geneticists spend the majority of their careers in the lab and therefore lack a sensitive bedside manner.

I watched Dr. Insufficient Social Graces conduct the entire exam with his back to me. Addressing the other physician, he rattled off Benjamin's physical characteristics. "Notice his head is small, thin upper lip, a high palate, and a slightly small chin. See his nipples? They are spread wide apart." I strained to look around the doctor's back to appreciate this observation. That was news to me. Was nothing sacred? I almost laughed, but then I thought about it. His nipples? *Thanks for pointing out one more abnormality, for scratching the lens with which I viewed my child.* I'd spend my entire life loving this boy, and I wanted to believe I could acclimate. How many times would I have to shift positions to see beyond the obstructions? Would they always be in my periphery?

I regretted taking a back seat while he treated my son like some lab rat. When I was a dance major, I studied biology with all the premed students. I was cornered by one in the lab, who demanded to know, "You're a dance major? Why are you taking biology?"

"It might surprise you that artists aren't exempt from completing core curricular requirements. I chose biology because I'd like to understand the human body. It is the instrument of my art. And the dance major requires rigorous academics."

"Oh, sure," he said with a wink.

"Listen," I said, "we have research papers and written tests as well as movement exams."

That got his attention. "You take written tests?"

Now as I sat behind the geneticist, I lost patience with his underestimation of my intelligence and my right to be included. At that point he was discussing genetic testing considerations with the visiting physician.

Pushing the obedient schoolgirl aside and wanting to place his arrogance under a hot spotlight, I said, "I think it's unnecessary to test the 17p13.3 chromosome. I know several children with that deletion. Benjamin's physical traits are inconsistent with Miller-Dieker syndrome."

Turning to face me with a flat affect, he insisted, "Only the test can rule out the diagnosis." I didn't agree with him, but I wasn't going to let my emotions stand in the way of acquiring factual data.

"Fine. Run the test, but it's going to be negative."

The results were negative, and we never saw him again.

When I was planning for parenthood, I never imagined how intimate we'd become with the field of medicine. I'll say this. I put my college studies in biology, psychology, anatomy, and kinesiology to good use. Before the age of two, in addition to his neurologist, Benjamin regularly saw an orthopedist to monitor tight muscle tone and skeletal problems and a gastroenterologist for reflux. He also needed a neuro-ophthalmologist to track his vision because of the seizure medication. As he got older, we added endocrinologists, pulmonologists, general surgeons, and rehabilitation specialists.

How naïve I was during pregnancy to think we'd only have to hunt for a pediatrician. Following the baby books to the letter, I organized a short list of practices that were close to our home, affiliated with a reputable hospital, had separate waiting rooms for sick and well children, and accepted our insurance. I chuckle at the image of myself thinking my biggest concern was finding a pediatrician who supported breastfeeding and our decision not to circumcise our son. John and I had researched and debated circumcision. In the end, we just didn't feel the need to change what nature had intended. We didn't want to use medical intervention without justifiable cause. So much of Benjamin's existence is still centered on questioning what is and isn't natural or necessary.

There were other geneticists who tried to take Benjamin's DNA apart. Their tests were equally unsuccessful in explaining the mysteries of Benjamin, but my dance degree had taught me to trust the language of movement over a doctor's labels. Years after I doubted the less severe PMG diagnosis, at least two other specialists agreed the severity of Benjamin's disabilities more closely represented lissencephaly.

While studying for my master's in special education, I learned it isn't always useful to take things apart. In the picture book *Seven Blind Mice* by Ed Young, an unknown creature confronts seven blind mice. The mice take turns meeting the creature, trying to figure out exactly what it is. The first six mice each make failed conclusions because they explore only one part of the being. The seventh mouse, however, takes the time to know the entire creature and therefore is able to properly define it. The book teaches an essential lesson. A teacher should not view a child in separate developmental pieces. Their cognitive skills can have an impact on their language and social development, for example. We must consider the whole child.

Benjamin was a whole child, not a collection of broken parts that needed fixing. He was who he was. The words of Benjamin's first and most hated neurologist rang true. "Benjamin is Benjamin. You should just love him." I understood what she meant. There's no difference between the child I brought to her and the one she diagnosed. He was simple to love, but that's not quite true. He was the same child, but I wasn't the same mother. Death is something I grew up fearing. Now that I'd linked death and Benjamin, I couldn't pull them apart, and yet I must.

Everywhere I looked, I found similar struggles. In our backyard, only two things managed to grow, the low-cut grassy weeds and a very old rosebush that refused to die, despite years of neglect. The bush grew around a tree stump. The stump constantly sprouted overbearing branches, twisting around and ruining the appearance of the rosebush. It was impossible to untangle the two conflicting elements without physically harming myself. In frustration, I once tried to kill the rosebush. I cut it down to the dirt in the middle of winter. It came back stronger, soft pink roses with thick thorns.

I often think of my friend's father who struggled with a degenerative muscle disorder for years. He developed a simple respiratory infection, except it exacerbated his already fragile body. As the illness progressed, doctors placed him on a respirator and inserted a feeding tube. It wasn't what he wanted. Although he knew his risk of death was high, he requested an extubation. As his family kept vigil, he tried to ease their pain. "Life is simple, but we make it complicated." I think he was quoting Confucius. I understand the statement, but I don't always agree.

We live. We love. We die. Hopefully, we live well, love deeply, and die peacefully. Sounds like the right fantasy, but what does any of it mean? How do we give up our heart, trust it to others, welcome a pain we never anticipated, and accept the simplicity in that? I did not make a choice to love Benjamin. I loved him from the moment I saw him. Perhaps before, but it wasn't the same. The point is there was never an option. My heart made demands my mind did not consider arguing with.

My father's heart attack was a simple event. One moment the muscle was working, and the next it wasn't. Simple, if you never care to ponder the why of it all.

Why a fatal heart attack on my brother's wedding day?

Why should motherhood hurt?

Am I simply allowing the pain to be?

These philosophical questions would never weigh Benjamin down. Should I be happy about that? How do I avoid these questions? It only seems to make sense if you take love out of the equation.

Simple mind = simple boy

Simple boy = simple life

But simple boy does not have simple needs

And complicated needs = complicated boy = complicated life

Would taking my heart out of the picture make it easier, or is it my mind that needs to get out of the way? The heart knows things before the mind. Why do we give an illogical organ such power? It can't think. But the mind can't think without a working heart. So the heart does have all the power. Doesn't the brain control the heart? The brain-dead would argue that point if they weren't brain-dead.

How do you love without thinking about how that love feels? When conflict cluttered my heart and brain, it was Benjamin who afforded me the ultimate retreat. I only needed to lie down next to him and look into his eyes. Ben was my Zen.

It had been a long and difficult first year, but Benjamin was seizure free. Two days before we celebrated Benjamin's first birthday, he was finished with the ACTH injections. His developmental progress was minimal, but that was no longer the top priority. He might not have been able to hold up his head, roll over, sit, stand, take one step, or use his hands, but he was alive. His presence was undeniably visible, an unexpected beauty in a dismal situation. I am forever adjusting my view of Benjamin and rosebushes.

5

Live in the Movement

A time to get, and a time to lose

The 1988 Hunter College Spring Concert had a total of eight dances. I performed in four of the pieces. The first was my own work, positioned fourth in the program, closing the first half of the show. It was an honorable placement, a spot typically reserved for strong work, giving the audience something to linger on. The next two ran back-to-back in the sixth and seventh spots, and after another intermission, *Time* was the finale. I was a senior enrolled in six classes, and I comanaged the dance company. All this in addition to the marathon of children's gymnastics classes I taught on Saturday mornings. I filled every day of those four months, and I wouldn't have wanted it any other way.

I loved performing, but it was easy to spiral into anxiety given all my responsibilities. Dance taught me how to manage even the greatest mental challenges. *What if I forget the choreography? What if I fall out of that turn or miss my mark or my entrance or fall behind or ahead of the music? What if I'm late after that quick costume change? Forget about last night's stupid cliché naked onstage nightmare. What if there's a lighting/music/prop mishap?*

Stop anticipating the worst outcomes. There's nothing to be afraid of. You've been working on this for months. You can adapt to anything.

Live in the Movement

Your body knows what it has to do. Stay out of your own way. Allow the movement to come naturally, without forcing it. And stop thinking about what the audience will think. Your friends and family are out there ready to support you. You'll be fine. Don't wish this all away. Slow down. Like Jim says, "Live in the movement." Meet each movement as it comes. Remember the way he glided his hands across the space in front of his body, as if he were touching the surface of water. Take the time to feel the space. Stay present. Enjoy the now because as soon as it's over, you're going to miss it.

In the summer after Benjamin's first birthday, we took our first family vacation to see the lissencephaly specialist in Chicago who had reviewed Benjamin's files and suggested the polymicrogyria (PMG) diagnosis. Seventeen months into this journey, we still felt our original questions were largely unanswered. John and I wrote a list of forty-three questions regarding the different types of neuronal migration disorders, causes, research, prevalence, prognosis, recurrence, prenatal testing, genetics, seizures, medications, and Benjamin's case history. Doctor's offices were a norm for us by then, but this pilgrimage to the guru of lissencephaly would help us determine whether or not to consider having more children.

Dr. Dobyns hung Benjamin's MRI scans on the lightboard. It wasn't the first time we had seen them, but it didn't matter. These were not the pictures I had been focusing on over the last few months. I looked back at Benjamin's trusting brown eyes. *Oh, my boy. I'm so sorry. How did this happen to you?* The images did not reflect anything that even vaguely resembled a typical brain. The reports were full of the medical terminology to describe his anomalies:

Microcephaly
Mild to moderately dilated ventricles

Fall *and* Recovery

Diffuse cerebral atrophy in the gray and white matter
Thinning of the cerebral gray matter cortex in association
    with a lack of sulcation
Deficient myelination

I avoided picturing Benjamin when I read the reports. The medical jargon was so alien it hardly seemed possible that it was describing my son. The scans made it unavoidable. The two sides of his brain were asymmetrical. Large, fluid-filled spaces occupied spots where brain matter should have been. The convolutions were unorganized. Dr. Dobyns traced a path across Benjamin's scan and added, "This is the perisylvian fissure. Your son's extends farther back than I've typically seen. My guess is there was a blood flow issue in the placenta. It probably happened around the thirteenth week of gestation. I don't see any calcifications, which means there aren't any signs of a prenatal infection."

I silently ran the checklist containing my top mommy guilt factors. I hadn't contracted any of the common infections to cause this. *That's good.* The placenta issue wasn't something I could ever control. *That's a problem.* I probed, "What about environmental causes? There was a terrible smell from the paint-stripping chemicals our neighbors were using, and then there's our old pipes."

He waved his hand. "There's no proof in my research to consider those as risks."

And then I asked the question we really needed answered. "What is the risk of having another child with PMG?"

"There's no evidence of a genetic mutation in Benjamin's blood work. The risk of recurrence in another pregnancy is possibly five percent. However, there could be an unknown genetic cause, and that would change the risk to one in four." I took no comfort in knowing we had a 75 to 95 percent chance of having a PMG-free child. We'd wrecked better odds than that when Benjamin was born.

Live in the Movement

Dr. Dobyns checked Benjamin's muscle tone, head control, and reflexes. We'd seen this so many times with scores of therapists and doctors that we'd numbed to what it all implied. A year earlier, I didn't think that was possible, and now watching another geneticist stepping out from behind his microscope to get his hands on what he would like to prove is the collective result of misshaped genes, better known to us as Benjamin, the pain felt new again. He was the top neuronal migration physician in the world; even a doctor from Italy concurred.

Dr. Dobyns laid out the future: "His overall delays suggest a risk for severe cognitive deficits. The foreseeable complications include eating problems, aspiration, repeated and life-threatening pneumonias, and with his severe spasticity, he'll have limited physical mobility. He needs a feeding tube. As far as life-span, he has a fifty percent chance of living to ten."

I stopped him there. "Benjamin eats by mouth. He still breast-feeds. Why does he need a feeding tube? Why ten?"

He explained, "Aspiration and pneumonia are what gets them. A feeding tube will help with that. In my experience, fifty percent of kids with G-tubes die in any given ten-year span. You'll have to decide whether you want to be aggressive by using available medical interventions such as feeding tubes, or take a care-and-comfort approach, treating his pain but not the underlying cause."

How could we live one day at a time, as the social worker insisted, and plan for the future?

Joanne, do not cry in front of this doctor. He's almost finished. Keep it together. Get Benjamin dressed and into his stroller. I gave John a look. *I'm done. Take it from here.*

As soon as Dr. Dobyns left, his assistant escorted us out. In a soft, caring tone, she said, "I know it's a lot to digest." My emotional dam broke. The tears streamed past my chin and soaked my shirt.

"Thank you," I said, pressing the back of my hand under my nose to stop a gush of fluid. "I'm sorry. I'm such a mess." *Dear God, will this well ever run dry?*

She handed me some tissues and said, "You can email or call if you have any questions or want to set up another appointment."

Mortality rates had never come up with Dr. Gold. Most doctors and therapists subscribe to the we-don't-have-a-crystal-ball mentality. Knowledge comes from experience with patients over time. As a teacher, I didn't try to make long-term assumptions about my students, nor did I focus on standardized norms. I guided each individual child through a series of sequential goals. It reminded me of gymnastics. You have to learn a forward roll before a handstand forward roll. Sure, the goal is to learn a front handspring, front tuck, but you have to build up to it with the basics. Special education is the same. There are long-term goals with several short-term goals in order to get there. The big goal is on the horizon while you focus intently on the individual step directly in front of you.

On our way back to the hotel, John asked, "What do you think about the feeding tube?"

"I don't like a fifty percent chance of death within ten years of getting a G-tube. Why would we do something so aggressive at this point? He doesn't need one, but if he suddenly couldn't eat well and was otherwise fine, we couldn't make him starve to death."

"No, I'm not saying we would do that."

"John, I don't know if I can make these types of decisions ahead of time. We have to wait and see what medical issues he develops. I just want Benjamin to be happy."

"He is happy. Let's keep focusing on giving him the best possible quality of life. As long as Benjamin is still Benjamin, we'll consider medical supports."

Every time I changed Benjamin's diaper, his intact foreskin

reminded me that we didn't want to change what nature had intended. We saved some skin. What would we be willing to give up in the years to come? How could we possibly live with making choices that could determine whether Benjamin lives or dies? Didn't that give us some false sense of control? We couldn't stop Benjamin from dying. The Internet parents shared very little about their children's final days. As much as I was curious to know what they'd been through, I didn't want to know what it looked like. I imagined it was like giving birth—sacred, private, and devastatingly beautiful.

Of course, we had already been making life-and-death decisions. The seizure medications could be deadly, but we lived the disclaimer: the benefits outweighed the risks. I wasn't sure if all the choices would be that obvious. I didn't like that level of responsibility or the feeling that we were playing God. Hard as it was, we would have to remember to be grateful for every happy and relatively healthy day Benjamin had. His happiness fueled my strength. Without it, I would have been lost and depleted.

During our time in Chicago, we visited a family from the Internet support group who lived nearby in Indiana. We were eager to meet another family in the flesh, but somewhat nervous. Their son, like other children with lissencephaly, had a feeding tube and a tracheostomy.

The parents showed us their kitchen. As an Italian, I've always viewed the kitchen as a place of magic, where loving hands transform simple ingredients, and unwritten family recipes connect one generation to the next. It's a place to gather and dip pieces of bread into a pot of tomato sauce simmering on the stove. No matter how small the space, Italians linger in the kitchen, nourished with food and laughter. In this home, disability infused the kitchen. "This is the feeding machine," the mom began. "We keep the syringes and tubes here on the counter. At night we put them in the dishwasher, then hang them on the cabinet handles to dry." I wasn't sure which seemed more displaced, the medical equipment or me.

I watched the mom suction her son's trach from time to time. I marveled at her matter-of-fact way of managing the medical devices. John and I exchanged glances throughout. I could tell we were of one mind thinking about quality-of-life issues. The definition of *quality* seemed hazy. I was abandoning the present and speeding ahead to an image of Benjamin without his vibrant personality and laughter. If Benjamin's health declined to the point of needing all this equipment, would our bond deteriorate? Could Benjamin still be Benjamin? These parents loved their son. They made difficult medical choices based on their unique understanding of his needs and adapted to a role of parenthood consumed with clinical caregiving. Even though it was the right thing for them, I wasn't certain John and I would make the same decisions. Does aggressive care mean extending a life not meant for survival? Does care and comfort mean letting your child die an unnecessarily premature death? Both paths seemed controversial. What would our friends, family, doctors, and the world think of us?

As we got ready to leave that evening, a thunderstorm hit. As we were saying our final goodbyes at the door, the house lost power. "Don't worry," the dad said. "This happens all the time. The backup generator will kick in." I stood frozen in the darkness. *Backup generator? We really are in the middle of nowhere. I would be terrified to live so far from the nearest neighbor or hospital.* The lights came on, and the mom added, "Why don't you stay a bit longer?"

I didn't give any serious thought to her suggestion. We needed to jolt ourselves back to our present reality.

"It's getting late. We should head back to the hotel and get Benjamin to bed."

Discussing medical interventions with Dr. Dobyns and seeing them in action were two different things.

We ran to the car and drove off, now realizing how fierce the storm was. The rain pounded the car, and we couldn't see two feet in front of us. The only moments of clarity came from the lightning strikes. One bolt revealed an otherwise invisible tractor-trailer in the intersection just ahead of us. Although John didn't need to hit the brakes, I still reached for the dashboard to brace myself. "Where the hell did he come from?"

John stared ahead, never showing trepidation.

"I could never drive in this type of rain. How can you stand it?"

"There's no place to pull over now."

"John, I can't wait till this ride is over."

"We'll get there."

"Not soon enough."

Benjamin was in the back seat roaring with laughter. Apparently, he loved the sound of the hard rain. I clung to his joy, always a comfort and my guide.

For the remainder of the trip, we focused on just being a family. It was something that often escaped us back at home. With no therapy schedule to adhere to, we explored zoos and museums. We took long walks, rode on amusement park rides, and took in a baseball game. We ate deep-dish pizza and a deep-dish chocolate chip cookie sundae I'll never forget. It almost felt normal. The summer winds of Chicago were strong and warm. I was a part of the world again.

Whatever was to come, our goals were clear. Because lifespan depended on the level of medical support a child needed, we would continue to seek out the smartest, most compassionate doctors and thoroughly committed therapists in an effort to stay ahead of foreseeable problems. We would tolerate nothing less from anyone who came into contact with our son. John and I were Benjamin's united advocacy team. It was time to go home and get on with life.

Benjamin was thriving in his own way. When I opened his

door every morning, he welcomed me with a smile. Nothing filled me more than the sight of him grinning, his eyes still closed. He loved the classic children's books *Goodnight Moon*, *The Runaway Bunny*, and *The Carrot Seed*. We could tell by his laughter and facial expressions that he had playlists of The Beatles and James Taylor memorized. He'd squeal and kick his legs with delight while watching me dance to his favorite tunes. His eyes would light up with anticipation when John hid behind his high chair and sneaked out to run circles around him. When he listened to our conversations, he always seemed to understand the jokes and laugh at the punch lines.

Benjamin took particular joy in seeing us do any type of manual labor around the house: mopping the floors, washing the dishes, collecting laundry. It was all one hysterical show. I think he was mocking me because, when I was pregnant, I often teased that he would one day do those things. He showed me. Gazing at him lying on his changing table, I had a strong sense that ten or twenty years ahead, Benjamin would still be the same, 100 percent dependent but happy. I envied his freedom from self-imposed negativity.

Despite Benjamin's happiness, I struggled whenever we saw a group of old friends. John has known this core group since middle school. My ex-boyfriend is among them. Doreen, my fourth-grade teacher, introduced us when I was a senior in high school. After dating for two years, I broke up with him shortly after I dropped out of college. John and I were nothing more than friends at the time. We connect with this group for all the major milestones: weddings, births, and annual get-togethers. There is comfort in familiarity, but I knew the next reunion would create some emotional challenges. Everyone had growing families, and all our children were close in age. Benjamin was the youngest.

Most of our friends had moved away from Brooklyn. This reunion took us to New Jersey. I stood with all the moms and marveled at the picturesque scene of children playing beneath the shade trees some thirty feet away.

"What a beautiful space for the kids," one mom said. "Could you imagine living here, Joanne?"

"No," I said as I shifted Benjamin from one shoulder to the other, taking in the space between him and the other children. "Don't get me wrong, it is beautiful, but we can barely take care of our twenty-by-twenty patch of grass in Brooklyn, and the taxes here are insane."

I had never dreamed of living in the suburbs. I'm a Brooklyn girl, but even if I wanted a change, nothing could begin to close the thirty-foot gap between Benjamin and the other boys and girls. Watching all those adorable little people exercising their budding independence filled my chest with an ache. I hugged Benjamin a little tighter and whispered, "I love you, Benjabeanie." It did little to quiet the conflict raging between my mind and my soul.

You have what you wanted, a child and a husband.

This isn't exactly what I wanted. I wanted what all our friends have. Is it so wrong to still want what they have? How did I end up so far from all my dreams? Where did I go wrong? Which choices did I screw up? Was it leaving dance and moving on to special education? I must have cursed myself. If I had stayed in dance, my whole life would be different. What if John and I are incapable of having a healthy child? Maybe I married the wrong man, and having a child with a disability is a sign that we don't belong together.

All right, now that's ridiculous. Just because your ex has a healthy son doesn't mean your life would have been better if you had stayed with him.

I know. John's the right man, but am I holding on to an unobtainable image of motherhood?

That baby you envisioned while meditating at the end of yoga class after your miscarriage is still floating somewhere in a cloud.

Is he really? Because I can't seem to touch him.

Sitting alone holding Benjamin—while the other moms moved around freely discussing homelife and work and fetching cocktails, and John was playing hacky sack with the other dads—my arms grew tired. I told myself what I'd told many of my students' parents. *Don't compare yourself or your child to anyone else. Concentrate on comparing Benjamin to Benjamin.*

My ex's wife joined me and offered to give me a break. As she cradled my eighteen-month-old son, she looked at me and said, "You know what he reminds me of? An infant."

It hit me like a right hook I didn't see coming. "I know" was the only polite response I could manage. Benjamin *was* like an infant, even had to be held like an infant. An eighteen-month-old infant. I just didn't need to hear it from her. *Joanne, I'm sure she just meant to express her affection for Benjamin's innocence and simple yet strong ability to exude love. It was just an innocent, unfiltered comment.* Sometimes that's all it takes to feel as though you're running in a dark, endless tunnel. I was plenty tired from the workout, and I wasn't seeing any forward progress. I felt empty.

I wanted to feel secure in the ever-cherished club of motherhood, but I had absolutely nothing in common with any of our friends. They were all loving and caring, but what could they really say or offer to keep me from fading into the hollowed shaft?

The laundry list of experiences I'd never have struck me. Benjamin couldn't walk. He couldn't talk. He couldn't play with the other kids. He wouldn't play in Little League like John had. He couldn't tell me where he hurt or if he had an itch. He couldn't tell me what he was thinking, ever. He couldn't call me Mommy or say I love you. He wouldn't grow up, go to college, move out, or get married and have his own kids. At future reunions, everyone would brag about their grandchildren, and Benjamin would be six feet under. I was on the bullet train to Cuckooville. When

I got Benjamin back in my arms, I looked into his Zen-full eyes. My brain slammed the brakes.

It was just another story to share with the Internet group about all the people in the world who just didn't get it. My Web counterparts had war stories of their own. I was angry, but I didn't know who or what to be angry at. Life had forced me to belong to this group, like a bad prearranged marriage. I didn't want any part of it, but I couldn't divorce it. Benjamin was my life. I wanted to be able to look at him without seeing this dehumanizing, diagnostic bubble around him. It's normal to go out on a quest to put a name to your child's disability. You need a medical diagnosis to justify therapy and medical intervention. You may even need it to feel like you belong. But when you get it, it threatens to strip your child of everything you thought was uniquely theirs.

I've seen numerous pictures of children with lissencephaly and PMG. They all look like Benjamin. He could very well be someone else's kid. What happened to all of our DNA? When I got pregnant, I wasn't preparing myself for an identity crisis or the blow to my ego. I rated myself fairly average in terms of intelligence. John was the nerdy kid who read the dictionary for fun and skipped eighth grade. Together, I thought we had a reasonable shot at having a bright child. I mean, have you taken a good look at some of the people who are out there procreating?

It's easy to spiral into anxiety and allow jealousy to get in the way of gratitude. These were my issues, not Benjamin's, and not our friends'. John's middle school buddies did what they could. During one reunion, we went to a local baseball game. When Benjamin wouldn't stop crying because the crowd's clapping and cheering was too loud for him (despite the fact that he was wearing earplugs), they all packed up their kids and left with us. No hesitation, no questions asked.

Benjamin had many challenges, but we tried to give him the

same experiences any other kid would have. It took a great deal of soul searching and modifications in order to do typical kid things without having all the typical expectations. At zoos and aquariums, we'd carry him so he could see things up close. We'd pry open his fingers and place objects in his hands. At the playground, we'd slide with him on our laps. When he was small enough, he could sit in the baby bucket swings if we propped him up with extra padding.

When he got taller, we scoped out the few parks that had an accessible swing. We'd often have to wait in the shade of all the nondisabled children whose families allowed them to occupy it first. I'd pace Benjamin back and forth, glaring at the parents. *Really? You don't see the disability sticker on the swing? You don't see this kid in the wheelchair waiting? How long are you going to let your perfectly normal, able-to-sit-in-one-of-the-other-five-swings child swing?* I'd give John an I'm-going-to-say-something-to-them look.

Blocking my path, he'd urge, "Joanne, don't. Just wait." I was tired of waiting for turns on swings, for heartache to pass, but zipping ahead didn't seem to be a solution either. I feared the injustices would grow right along with Benjamin, and life would always find a way of setting us apart.

Use Oppositional Forces to Maintain Balance

*A time to plant, and a time to pluck up
that which is planted*

One of the reasons I love modern dance is because it thrives on breaking rules. Traditional ballet is centuries old with limited and strictly defined movement expressed through French terminology. Arms and feet have specific, numbered positions. A ballerina pulls up away from the ground and must achieve balance on the smallest of foundations, at the tip of a pointe shoe.

During my Hunter days, I experimented with dance classes throughout Manhattan and found a beginner ballet class given by a well-respected Frenchman. I stood with the other dancers at the barre performing a basic tendu exercise. Standing in first position (legs straight, heels together, toes facing outward, stomach in, and buttocks tight), I shifted my weight over to my left leg and glided my right foot out to the side. Once my right foot reached a fully extended, pointed position, I relaxed my toes, squeezed and glided my right leg back to the starting first position.

The teacher banged his cane on the floor and yelled, "Stop!" to both the dancers and pianist. I held my breath as he walked toward me. *Did I shift my weight too far to the left the way my modern teachers instructed?* He addressed the ballerina behind me: "Show me a tendu." Squatting down, he investigated the movement of her foot. "No, no, no. Take off your slipper. No, like this," he said as he manipulated her foot to the side and adjusted the path and position of her third toe. As he walked away, he asked, "How long have you been dancing?"

The ballerina replied, "Ten years." All of her toes looked fine to me. If she was still trying to perfect the placement of her third toe in a tendu after ten years of training, I didn't have a prayer.

Later in class, away from the barre, the teacher gave a pirouette exercise. "Start in first, tendu right, plié fourth, passé, relevé, pirouette en dehors." I marked the movement in place as he spoke without fully performing the task. A moment later, I assumed first position and reviewed the movement in my head as I awaited the cue to start.

Squeeze your legs together. Stretch up tall and close your ribs like you're wearing a corset. Maintain a rounded shape with your arms as if you're holding a full basket. Don't tip your pelvis. Tendu right, open arms, ribs closed, reach up through the top of your head. Step back and bend your knees, right arm front, ribs closed. Swing your right arm open and snap your left arm like a slamming door, bring the left ribs around, hold your basket. Snap up high on your left foot, right foot to the left knee. Keep your ribs closed. Spot the front of the room. Stretch your body up.

If I were singing the ABC song, I would complete the pirouette by the letter *G*. Under the watchful eye of a perfection seeker such as the Frenchman, that was more than enough time to berate myself. *You're leaning back. You're off-balance. Don't drop your left heel until the rotation is complete.* The teacher paced in front of the class and once again spoke to Ms. Misaligned Third Toe. "Well," he said, raising his cigarette in the air before taking a long drag. "I think that you love dance, but I do not think that dance loves you." After a decade of ballet classes, I suppose she'd habituated to this type of degradation because she said nothing and showed no emotion. I hid my desire to run behind a stone-cold look on my face, but there's no hiding in ballet.

The teacher looked at me. "How long have you been dancing?"

"Two years," I said.

"Really. Hmmmm."

My inexperience helped me to escape his public criticism, but ballet was like Catholic school, full of harsh judgment with an expectation of rigid conformity and always certain to make me feel like I was never good enough.

Modern dance emerged in the late 1800s with an unlimited movement vocabulary. Modern dancers use gravity as a friendly force. They are free to fall. The floor is a foundational partner, used to support and power movement. You go down to go up, like a human handball. Dancers find balance in any and every conceivable position.

In "A Time to Laugh," I ran around in circles giggling. I looked for classmates backstage making funny faces at me. Laughter led my body down to the ground and rolled me back up. Overcome with laughter, I bent forward as if hanging from an imaginary string on my back, wrapped my arms in front of me while spinning on my bent left leg, and swung my right leg back feeling the full force of my weight going down into the floor. Still spinning, I swung my torso and arms up to the sky. A big breath of air helped me to stretch straight up through my left leg as I swung my right leg forward. Landing sideways on parallel feet, looking out toward the audience, I completed two quick jumps. Then I bent forward, wrapped my arms in front of me, and duplicated the double turn in the opposite direction on my right leg. The choreography specified the placement of my legs, torso, and arms, but based on the mechanics of my body, there was room for adaptation.

Some would argue that a single pirouette in ballet class is easier than a double turn moving from one extreme body position to another. My body begged to differ. While both dance techniques required imagining a stable axis through the body, modern placed equal value on the use of oppositional forces and created an opportunity to embrace imbalance.

When John and I decided to get married, he searched for a ring at our favorite antique jewelry store in downtown Manhattan. Located steps away from the hustle of the subway and the anything goes mentality of the West Village, the store was a cozy world of old, reliable gems. To his surprise, John didn't like any of the engagement rings and decided to search beyond antiques. "I found a ring," he announced, "but I'm not sure you'll like it. It's not an antique."

"What is it? Where's the store?"

"It has a modern setting. I found it in a store on Madison Avenue."

"Madison Avenue? You want me to walk into some uppity, posh jewelry store on Madison Avenue? Look at us. We're jeans and T-shirts people. We don't fit in there."

I was more than intimidated when I walked down the carpeted center strip lined with lights guiding me past pillars topped with plexiglass boxes of expensive, shiny new rings, but John had found something so unique I couldn't resist.

The ring had a diamond suspended within a platinum band, stabilized only by tension. Most people couldn't believe the diamond was secure, but I completely respected the oppositional forces that supported it. I didn't need a diamond like everyone else that seemed artificially held in place against its will. Although tension supplies the balance, air and light surround the diamond with little inhibition. It is not static. There is an implication of movement. I liked the idea of something inanimate being so organic.

My life had plenty of tension, but unlike my diamond ring, I was still seeking a balance.

When Benjamin grew out of his baby carriage, we started using a large adaptive stroller. I'd cringe at every restaurant or specialty store that posted "No Strollers Allowed" signs. I have a thing about following rules. I come to a full stop at stop signs on deserted roads in the dead of night. I don't even like crossing the street mid-block. Certainly, common sense and personal desire have swayed me, but it makes me uncomfortable, especially when someone is watching me.

Well-meaning store employees have a thing about following rules too, and they'd eagerly stop us.

"I'm sorry, miss; there are no strollers allowed."

"It's not a stroller. It's a wheelchair."

Sometimes they'd step aside. "I'm so sorry. I didn't realize." Other times they'd apologize about the rules as they kicked us out. Either way, I'd curse them, sometimes out loud, and push Benjamin into the world of parents with their children who walked, talked, and swung in the only playground swing my son could use.

At least by then, Benjamin's early intervention team had helped us transplant ourselves into the local disability community. One of the challenges of being a special educator is helping children and parents through program transitions. As difficult as it can be at first to accept the need for early intervention services, it is a family-based service. The older a child gets, the less family-centered the services become. I had grown to love Benjamin's home therapists. Nothing gave me a greater sense of purpose or the ability to get through a day like those scheduled appointments.

The speech therapist encouraged me to build on Benjamin's strong eye contact. As a precursor to verbal communication, we modeled different sounds and looked at him expectantly in hopes he'd reciprocate. We'd place small amounts of food in different parts of his mouth to improve tongue mobility and used vibrating toys to encourage lip closure. The physical and occupational therapists would coax Benjamin's stiff limbs to move more freely, giving him better awareness of his body. Switch-activated toys allowed him to make the cow moo, the pig oink, and the giraffe walk. We had massive equipment cluttering our one-hundred-year-old Victorian house to help Benjamin crawl, sit, stand, and walk. Even though Benjamin never accomplished any of these skills, the therapists were committed to helping our family fit into a world that no longer demanded institutionalization but lacked sufficient inclusionary opportunities.

Right before Benjamin turned two, the early intervention director recommended that, in addition to home-based services, we place Benjamin in a center-based program where only children with disabilities were in attendance. I tried to imagine waking him up every morning and sending him off to school. How could I monitor what happened to him? It wasn't like he could tell me about his day. I could see the benefit of more services, but could Benjamin handle school all morning plus therapy at home all afternoon? Could I handle the thought of other people taking care of him when I wasn't there? How would Benjamin handle a classroom filled with other children? Sudden loud noises still startled him and could possibly bring on seizures.

Despite my hesitation, John and I toured a local program, housed in an old Catholic school building. The stone floors and dark wooden doors brought back memories of my grammar school days at St. Charles Borromeo in Brooklyn Heights. Unlike John, who went to public schools, I wasn't educated alongside students classified with disabilities. There was an adult disability program affiliated with St. Charles, housed in a building on my block.

Use Oppositional Forces to Maintain Balance

Sometimes when I played outside with friends after school, a bus would drop off program participants. They walked choppily and made unpredictable, loud noises. They scared me.

With Benjamin on my lap, we sat in the office exchanging glances with two moms sitting across the way. *What on earth am I doing here? He's too little for school. How do parents put a two-year-old on a school bus?*

The classrooms reminded me of my days at work before Benjamin. Inside, teachers and assistants read stories, sang songs, passed out snacks, and wiped little hands and noses. There were children who independently explored books and toys, and others who played seated in adaptive chairs. We met a nurse who shared Benjamin's birthday. Therapists worked with kids in the halls, classrooms, and in a therapy room complete with mats, inflatable gym balls, and swings. There were lots of smiling faces, and no shortage of hugs and kisses for the students. It seemed unfair to keep Benjamin from such a warm environment. I would just have to push my fears aside in order to give him the quality of life he deserved. Isn't that what John and I had agreed to in Chicago? Quality of life, once again redefined.

The bus, however, was nonnegotiable. I drove him every day and made friends with those moms who remembered Benjamin sitting in the office with his brown bomber jacket and long eyelashes. We'd drop off our babies, head out to breakfast, and share stories about our isolated lives, instantly making them less so. It was a perfect supplement to the Internet support group.

I didn't anticipate it, but I found something stabilizing about being in a community where I didn't have to make excuses or feel awkward about my child. It was a place where the playing field was level. Every family walked our path, but there was always someone whose shoes we would rather not be in. My new personal mantra: No matter how bad things seem, it could always be worse. I don't know how, but it could always be worse.

In this school, all I had to do was look around if I really wanted to appreciate my life. The mothers were as varied as their children's disabilities, and I found the true essence of the word *hero*. It is the mother of four who barely slept because her daughter woke constantly and, left unsupervised, might punch herself repeatedly. It is the mother who watched her daughter come back from death more than once. It is the mother who stifled her own panic disorder in order to defend her daughter against strangers who told her she shouldn't be out in public. It is the mother who in fact buried a daughter and still managed to expand her family. It is every single one of those mothers who loved their children more than they loved themselves. We formed our own breakfast club and were safe together.

When I participated in Jim's memorial at Hunter, we focused on the intangible gifts Jim had left behind. Gifts death could never take away. Within the walls of Benjamin's school, the children's unique and intangible gifts never went unnoticed. I watched in wonder as Benjamin grew to love this new environment. He was suddenly doing the impossible, finding a way to be independent of me. He loved all the attention and was an incredible flirt. He made strong connections to his teachers and especially to his personal aide, Anna.

Benjamin was learning the art of manipulating others. The moment Anna would walk away, Benjamin would cry, and she would come running back. He could flip a cry into laughter in a millisecond. At home we dubbed him "the master of the laugh/cry." He would try to use this technique to weasel out of therapies. Therapists often banned Anna from therapeutic sessions because Benjamin wouldn't listen to anyone else in her presence. He knew how much Anna loved him, and so did I. He would come home every day smelling of her perfume, which meant she had been holding him for long stretches of time.

One day, his teacher pulled me aside to inform me that

Use Oppositional Forces to Maintain Balance

Benjamin had spoken his first word. "From across the room, he yelled out, 'Anna.'" I didn't believe her, but the entire classroom staff insisted. So, I lovingly told my son that he was a traitor. My mother insisted he actually said, "Nana." It was just so satisfying to see the effect he was having on people outside our family. His home-based early intervention team seemed especially taken by that beautiful pure sense about him. Everyone fell in love with him—his wide smile, hardy laugh, beautiful thick curly hair, and long eyelashes were hard to resist.

As his transition progressed, I received an unexpected call from the early intervention director. "Now that Benjamin's in school, we'd like you to come work for us as an early intervention provider."

"I've never taught infants and toddlers," I said. "I only took one early intervention class in college. My experience is with pre-schoolers, and I haven't taught for two years."

She was undeterred. "What do you think you've been doing with Benjamin all this time?"

It was time to stretch my abilities. Benjamin's home-based therapists had been such a positive support to our whole family. It would be immensely rewarding if I could manage to be a genuine resource to others. In the center-based preschool where I had worked years earlier, I rarely got to interact with the parents. With my new perspective, I hoped to be a more effective educator.

One of my first clients was an infant with hypotonic cerebral palsy. He had an older sibling with a disability. The idea of a second child was still active in my mind, and this family's reality disheartened me. During our first phone conversation, the mother detailed her son's birth story, the moment when suspicions arose, the confirmation of diagnosis, and the phone calls to secure intervention. I swallowed the knot in my throat, realizing she had more experience in early intervention than I did. When I arrived on the family's doorstep, armed with a massive bag of infant toys and preperformance-like jitters, I questioned my ability to provide an entire hour of meaningful therapy.

I rang the bell, rattling off affirmations inside my head as I waited. *You can do this. You don't have any problems engaging Benjamin all day.*

But my nerves had nothing to do with lesson plans or time management. *Can I look this mother in the face without seeing myself? Could this happen again to me?*

Special educators often talk about teaching students to generalize information. Once a child has mastered a skill in the classroom, the next step is teaching them to perform the same skill in different environments. I was set to generalize the lessons I had learned, as a parent of a child with a disability, and apply them to my role as a teacher.

I thought about the simple things Benjamin's providers did to make our experiences positive, like arriving on time so Benjamin's feeding and sleep schedules went uninterrupted. Having a therapist come into your home is meant to be a great support, and it is, but it can also be incredibly invasive. It was difficult for me to depend on a series of strangers to give my child something I couldn't provide. Something I wished he never needed. I had to find the balance between helping and intruding.

The best therapists understood our whole family. They respected our knowledge but educated us without being pretentious. I could forget my fears by focusing on this family's unique circumstances and concerns. I headed back to the developmental milestone books I had come to despise during Benjamin's first months. My approach was structured and sequential. I built teaching strategies by organizing my resources and drawing from my personal foundation. One of Benjamin's classmates also had hypotonic cerebral palsy. I relied on her mother's insight. Early development is heavily motoric. So I combined what I had learned from Benjamin's OT and PT about movement patterns with my years of knowledge as a gymnast and dancer. I knew muscle and skeletal anatomy, and how to teach movement from one foundational skill to the next. I knew how to use my hands to support and guide a child's body. Then I also combined what I'd learned about early language development from Benjamin's speech therapist with the unique understanding dance afforded me about nonverbal communication. I knew how to listen to and interpret movement and behavior through careful observation, and how to connect through my actions without relying on words.

This baby boy deserved the same level of effort everyone had given Benjamin. I had no doubt his gains would surpass my son's. Even though I knew Benjamin's lack of progress was not controllable, it had made me question my ability as an educator, but this tiny baby boy with floppy muscle tone restored my faith. I watched him slowly and steadily make those gains Benjamin had missed. I worked with him long enough to see him stand. It was a gift. I was the recipient.

I treated each new client with the same drive. Books on chromosomal disorders, brain malformations, and environmental neglect lined my shelves. I listened to the parents. I heard their fears. I felt their pain. It wasn't always easy to balance my emotions. I can't watch another person cry without ending up in a puddle myself. The parents' despair was still very much my own. I tried to provide a sense of empowerment by teaching families how to be advocates, whether it was asking for additional services or navigating the local playground.

Raising a child with disabilities is complicated and fulfilling all at once. I spent years in Catholic school learning how it isn't nice to judge others. That's what they taught, but it's not what they did, and I learned the lesson they modeled. Human beings judge other human beings. It's normal, but early intervention taught me to judge my assumptions.

Fall *and* Recovery

Parents of children with disabilities are typecast. We are defensive and overbearing, or anxious and overwhelmed. We are keen and controlling, or fragile and sad. Our parenting skills are either too permissive or authoritarian. We're religious, medicated, forever on a paid couch, or just plain crazy. When I worked as an early intervention provider, I saw parents where they lived: dressed and ready to take on the world or unwashed and in their pajamas. There was no hiding spousal fights, or the fact that the baby had been up all night, or an illness in the family. I gained a greater perspective and learned to think and treat others with greater compassion.

Parents live with constant uncertainty, and everything can hold an unrealistic weight. I agonized over choosing a preschool with the intensity of a cardiac patient deciding on a surgeon. I wish I had realized sooner that sometimes there are no perfect answers. It's a lesson I try to share, as much as possible, with other parents. When things don't work out as hoped, it's not a matter of having made some egregious mistake. There's no guarantee that different choices would have yielded more positive outcomes. We do what we are capable of at any given time. What more can you expect of yourself?

Classroom teachers only know what they see and what families are willing to tell them. I had an advantage over other therapists. The parents knew I sat on their side of the table, and it allowed them to confide in me more readily. They knew, like I knew, the difference between someone who "gets it" and someone who never could. I've been both of those people.

In my first year of teaching in the self-contained special education preschool, I had a student whose mother wrote me an angry letter because her daughter came home with messy hair and shoes on the wrong feet. All preschool children get messy and put their shoes on wrong. I couldn't understand her anxiety. I see it differently now. Perhaps she thought messy hair or improperly worn shoes would make her daughter stand out. Maybe she didn't want to draw attention to her child's disability. I think I dressed Benjamin to perfection in hopes of keeping strangers from staring for too long.

Disabled or not, perfection is nothing but a time-wasting, soul-sucking illusion. When I was in kindergarten, I threw a total hissy fit upon discovering I'd made a mistake on a home-work coloring assignment. I can still hear the scraping of the knife I insisted my mother use to remove the improperly placed wax. Even a simple act like buttering toast was a major event. I needed an absolutely even layer of fat on my perfectly toasted white bread. Clumps were not acceptable, and every centimeter of the non-crusted part of the bread had to be covered. I have spent my entire life trying to balance this innate rigidity with my strong creative drive.

Teaching requires structure and creativity. If you're going to stand in front of a class for six hours, you need to entertain. If you're going to sit with babies working on the same skill for months at a time, you need to make repetition fun. If you want to motivate parents to work with their children to reinforce your work, it better not seem like an assignment.

Unfortunately, the early intervention system in New York started making changes I didn't like. In the beginning, I provided service directly to the child. Then there was a shift to a parent-train-ing model. I fully appreciate the theory that teaching a parent the skills to help their child is empowering. Every family has to learn how to manage their child's needs and how to encourage growth. Benjamin's therapists modeled everything I needed to be a better parent and a better teacher, but I didn't have to bear the responsi-bilities of each separate therapist. Most parents become extremely proficient at delivering therapeutic care, but in their own time. I began to lose faith in a system that required me to present parents with a monthly calendar on which I had written daily activities for them to complete. They had to mark the calendar with a plus or minus sign to indicate the effectiveness of the strategies.

When Benjamin was five months old, I needed someone to lighten my daily load. His EI team did that for me. They didn't give me homework. Calendars hold such significance. I had a commercial "baby's firsts" calendar, but I stopped using it when Benjamin had no gains to report. I still don't like to look at it. It's a permanent written marker of exactly when Benjamin's future as I had imagined it was lost.

Fortunately, Benjamin aged out of early intervention before I was required to place those plus or minus signs on a calendar made just for him. On the other hand, I dreaded Benjamin's transition from the combination center-based, home-based early intervention services to center-based-only preschool services. Benjamin's home-based therapists had been a daily part of our lives for three years. It was like losing family, but I was fortunate to keep many of them in my life as colleagues and friends. Our support had shifted, but our resources were intact. Benjamin's transition to preschool was seamless because he stayed in the same school. He simply had a longer school day with all his therapies provided there.

Past the highs and lows of Benjamin's early intervention and preschool transitions, John and I prepared to enjoy an uneventful two years before the move to kindergarten. I felt a calm that had evaded me since Benjamin's first week of life. At age thirty-five, it was time to revisit the original family plan: two children by the time I was thirty-five. John and I weighed the information Dr. Dobyns had given us in Chicago. The numbers seemed to be in our favor, but more importantly, we wanted to trust the doctor's instincts. I couldn't imagine that a problem with the placenta would happen again, but I was afraid that my desire for another child was blinding my judgment.

We sought out an unbiased opinion from a high-risk OB-GYN. We showed up with stacks of medical records in hand and made it clear we wanted every available prenatal test to screen for anything even vaguely resembling PMG. An abortion was not something I wanted to experience in my life, but John and I didn't think it would be fair to make another child suffer, and we worried that having two children with disabilities would compromise our ability to care for either one of them. Although she understood our concerns, she felt confident that a subsequent pregnancy would not qualify as high-risk. She cited wishful thinking: "Lightning never strikes twice."

I certainly hoped not, but Mother Nature is a notorious rule breaker.

Part Two

Static

Pain Is the Messenger

A time of war, and a time of peace

On the day Benjamin was born, my mother wrote me a letter:

To My Beloved Daughter,

Today is a very special day. Today you become a mom. This is my seventh grandchild, but to me this child is especially more precious because my baby is having her baby. I know you will be a great mother. I wish for you that your child will make you as proud and happy as you have made me.

Love this child!

Listen to this child!

Be there, for time goes by and before you know it, you will be right here where I am today. Waiting for your grandchild.

No. I wouldn't. As much as John and I loved Benjamin and enjoyed every moment possible, there would always be a part of us that was injured. I just wanted to experience motherhood without all the extraordinary medical responsibilities. I wanted a lifetime of that blissful first week we had after he was born. I wanted what my mother and every other mother in my family had, the ability to pass on traditions. Benjamin had made them all seem so irrelevant. I wanted to raise a child, to see him reach adulthood and do something he loved. I didn't want to come to the end of my life, having buried my only child, and have that as my legacy.

The day after Benjamin was born, I took a picture of John kneeling next to his newborn son in the hospital bassinet. John looks tired but beaming with pride. It's a look only a new father has: a pure expression filled with an obscene amount of love and appreciation for life. One-day-old Benjamin had given John something he was lacking. Unadulterated optimism. When I look at that image of my husband now, I see how much he loves that baby, and I know all the grief that is yet to come. I feel useless because I can't take away that impending pain. We can never recapture the innocence that existed the day that photo was shot.

Before we lived together, I thought John was an easygoing, confident guy, but I came to see his basic view of life is pessimistic. No matter what he accomplishes, he sees himself as a loser. He expects that life will target him for punishment. He only shows this side of himself to me. It was so unfair that fatherhood fed his insecurities.

John once confessed that, although we'd discussed and agreed on raising two children, he would have been happy without any. Whether it was marriage, his friend's children, or just climbing aboard my dream, John embraced fatherhood. Before Benjamin was born, I'd guess John's initial fantasies revolved around playing baseball and sharing his love of movies with his children. For Benjamin, John replaced his fantasy of playing catch with manipulating adapted toys. He spent his weekends holding Benjamin in his arms and sleeping on the floor next to his crib, one arm wedged between the bars, holding Benjamin's hand. He logged an obscene number of hours watching *Clifford* and the *Teletubbies*.

With no time to waste on my thirty-five-year-old clock, John and I tossed our fate to the wind. Over-the-counter ovulation test kits provided me with the illusion of control over a fate that was utterly independent of my organizational skills, and they worked as advertised. In just two months, I was staring at the double pink lines on a pregnancy test stick. I called my high-risk OB-GYN to arrange the first prenatal appointment. The secretary searched for openings. "You can come in in four weeks."

Four weeks is an eternity when you want to confirm the stability of a pregnancy, but it isn't like the doctor could do anything for me. Whether or not the pregnancy would hold was up to nature. At just four weeks along, I didn't feel pregnant, which concerned me. It might seem strange that I expected to notice the existence of an embryo the size of a poppy seed, but as John likes to say, "You're so sensitive to your body." It's true. Dance trained me to listen to my body and notice the slightest changes. At the four-week mark of my other pregnancies, my breasts were tender and tingling, and I couldn't get through the day without a nap. With this pregnancy, I felt nothing out of the ordinary. Was this even real? John and I weren't sure if we should share the news with anyone before we saw the doctor, in case of another miscarriage.

My first pregnancy loss marked the start of a dark motherhood. I can smell the flowers John brought for me. I can't remember what they looked like, but in the days after the miscarriage, their death was pungent. It was the first bouquet he'd ever purchased for me and the last for several years to come. In my closet, I buried a set of gold hoop earrings John's sister bought for me after we'd announced the pregnancy. After the miscarriage, I tried to give them back, but Nina refused. "You keep them." I couldn't wear them. They reminded me of what I'd lost. Golden hoops were a poor substitute for the brass ring I just couldn't reach. I could plan, I could aim, but I didn't always get what I thought I deserved. This had been true in motherhood and dance. I had few tangible mementos from my life as a dancer. After two pregnancies, I had one adorable disabled child with a shortened life expectancy. Now that I was pregnant again, I wondered if our friends and family would think it was absurd for us to want another child.

My body really hated being pregnant. The nausea began six weeks in. Benjamin found it hilarious whenever I got the heaves. Perhaps it was my mad dashes to the nearest toilet or sink that got him laughing. I had hoped I wouldn't feel so physically miserable again. I cracked open the door of anxiety. *Can I do this? Too late now, Joanne. It's already done.*

Perpetual morning sickness slowed every day down. No matter how many times I stared at my calendar, that first appointment seemed far off. I counted and recounted the days as if I would come across a mistake in my math. John couldn't break away from work to come to the first prenatal visit. I tried not to be an irrational, hormonal knocked-up wife. With his current schedule, I was lucky to be pregnant at all. Just because the little hormone stick says it's time to procreate doesn't guarantee your husband is in the mood when he only has four hours a night to sleep. As much as I wanted to share the first visit with John, I didn't want to argue about it.

On the day of the appointment, my body tensed as Dr. Patrick wheeled the sonogram equipment my way. I held my breath and stared at the monitor as she placed the wand on my abdomen. In the center of the blackness, there it was. Pointing to the screen, she said, "Do you see the heartbeat? It's strong." I lay mesmerized by the pulsing movement, the proof that a baby was thriving within me. A baby who was tapping into every cell and function of my body, and whose heartbeat created a rhythm I longed to connect with. I gazed at this baby, so small and so big, because I wanted to believe that this still intangible miracle would change everything for the better.

Handing the sonogram picture to me, Dr. Patrick added, "Let's do the amniocentesis as early as we can. And have you go for additional sonograms with a fetal brain specialist." Nodding, I focused on the photo. *Dear God, I know I've questioned, complained, lost faith in the church, and even doubted your existence, but I've done my best to live with and learn from every difficult situation, from my father's death to Benjamin's diagnosis. While I've struggled to find gratitude in your steering me from dance to special education, I know the change primed me for my life with Benjamin. I am doing my best, but I need your help. Please let this baby bring John and me some peace.* I put a lot of faith in the promise captured on a flimsy strip of paper.

I was relieved to receive a steady outpouring of love and support from everyone. Even Benjamin's neurologist's secretary was excited. She was always pleasant at our appointments with Dr. Gold, but a full-out glowing smile was a clear departure from her cool, levelheaded demeanor. As much as everyone embraced Benjamin, I wondered if they thought a new child would bring us closure, acceptance, recovery.

On the day of the amnio, John and I watched the sonogram images as Dr. Patrick inserted the needle. The shape of the baby's head looked more symmetrical than Benjamin's. We saw a hand moving up toward the face as the mouth opened awaiting a thumb. I squeezed John's hand. He squeezed back. This four-month-old fetus could already do things that three-year-old Benjamin couldn't. It was a sad yet reassuring realization.

After ten long days, the results came back normal, and we were having another boy. Ever practical minded, I thought about all the bins of Benjamin's infant clothes and the money we would save on a wardrobe. Ever sentimental, I thought about the freedom of movement each garment had lacked when Benjamin wore them. John and I were relieved but guarded about the results. After all, Benjamin's amniocentesis had been normal.

An amnio screens for a limited number of disorders. As advanced as the world of genetics had grown by 2002, medicine still had its limitations. Doctors could only test for a defect if they knew where to look for it. There were maybe a handful of known indicators for neuronal migration disorders. The bizarre alphabet jungle that makes up our DNA hides some genetic mishaps exceptionally well. If doctors hadn't been to that section of the wilderness, they didn't really know if it existed. It makes me think of the old philosophical question about the tree falling in the forest. If no one is around to hear it, does it make a sound? Does it matter?

The way I see it, the existence of the fallen tree is only relevant if it causes a chain reaction and the final tree to fall lands on your house. On the other hand, I have a strong belief that all living things share a connection and influence each other through a sequence of interactions well beyond our sight and imagination. I developed this idea during a dance rehearsal at Hunter. I was being lazy, marking my steps instead of dancing full-out. With one misstep, I sprained my ankle. An injury in one joint can affect even the most distal, seemingly unrelated body part. In an effort to compensate for the initial injury, a chain of subtle adjustments can occur. The foot throbs, the calf tightens, the thigh and hip spasm. The spine makes for an obvious conduit. The vertebrae at the top of the line, already overburdened by the job of supporting the head, struggle to oppose the forces of each individual physical mismanagement. Pain is not something to ignore. Pain is a messenger, not an enemy. Compensating for an injury is not the recommended strategy in the healing process.

While it was easy to admit that motherhood had injured a deep part of my being, I didn't want to see a new baby as compensation. I didn't expect closure, acceptance, or recovery because no perfectly healthy child could change Benjamin's fate. I hadn't allowed myself to realize my pain could spread and Benjamin, alive or dead, would influence the way I move through the rest of my life, and not always in a healthy manner.

Pain Is the Messenger

I'd hoped to feel an ounce of reassurance that this baby was not like Benjamin, but the prenatal similarities were distracting, especially the continued nausea and the first visual movement at seventeen weeks. When analyzing the frequency and quality of every movement didn't relieve my anxieties, I hyperfocused on the scientific facts. My high-risk OB and a fetal brain specialist probed and scanned me every few weeks. I ended up with nine pages of sonogram pictures, all with normal reports.

Halfway through the pregnancy, in the middle of summer, John left for a three-and-a-half-month gig in Charleston, South Carolina. Fourteen weeks in pregnancy time was forever on my calendar. John didn't travel often, but working freelance in film, he didn't always have an option. You follow the work or go without a paycheck. Having John home on a hiatus was tempting, but with my maternity leave approaching, it was not a luxury we could afford.

As John packed, we discussed the things that made it easier to say goodbye but we knew would never happen. He could make some weekend trips home. I could bring Benjamin down to Charleston for a family vacation. Neither made any financial sense, and I couldn't handle the travel. Before John left, he took a couple of pictures of me to document the size of my belly. All I saw in those photos were my swollen red eyes, forever marking John's imminent departure. He landed seven hundred plus miles and a lifestyle away.

As the next four weeks passed, I grew fatter and more emotional. My early intervention caseload included two families living in un-air-conditioned, fourth-floor walk-ups. Those massive bags of infant toys I traveled with didn't help. Neither did Benjamin's daily care. Every week got a little tougher. At three and a half years old, Benjamin still needed complete support for feeding, dressing, bathing, and diapering. I was concerned about lifting him for every transition, but my doctor wasn't. Benjamin was light. It wasn't an issue of his weight. We lived in a row house with plenty of stairs. I constantly worried I would take a fall with him in my arms.

I missed John. I stood in his closet, between his shirts, to feel him surround me. Closing my eyes, I'd breathe in his scent. Even though in the height of his production schedules he was barely home long enough to lie down next to me, I liked knowing he was present. I found comfort in the sound of his morning shower and the one kiss he'd plant on my barely conscious head when he left for the day. I really thought I could handle his absence.

Benjamin seemed unfazed, which is exactly what John had feared.

"He's going to forget me."

"He won't forget you. He cries every time you walk out of the room and laughs as soon as you come back." Was I wrong? How could Benjamin forget all the hours his father held him on his lap? Somewhere in Benjamin's fibers, he had to miss his father. Part of me wanted time to speed up, to bring John home. Part of me wished time would completely stop, to keep things the same before all of the unknowns would come to be. I especially didn't want to reach the end of the pregnancy feeling as though I had kept myself from enjoying the experience.

I needed some serious pampering, and there was only one person who could do it: my mother. For the last three weeks of summer, she cooked all the meals and let me sleep late in her one-level, centrally air-conditioned home. Benjamin and his grandma have an inspiring connection. Whenever he sees her, he thrusts his legs as if he could run and laughs uncontrollably as she habitually speaks with her hands. Indeed, it was exactly what I needed in order to sit back and appreciate the moment. What was the harm in counterbalancing John's absence with my mother's help? I didn't actually believe the presence of one person could compensate for the lack of another, although my family has a history of believing in such ridiculous notions.

Pain Is the Messenger

On the day I was born, my father was at his brother's funeral. My widowed aunt flatly acknowledged my arrival. "Well, one goes out and one comes in." My brother John's life, filled with bittersweet events, carries on this compensatory myth as well. First, it was my father's death on his wedding day. Then, his father-in-law died on my birthday. His mother-in-law died on his birthday. Our stepfather died on his daughter's birthday. Only once did he break the happy/tragic day legacy. His son Evan was born on my birthday. I hoped to do the same. My new little one was due on my nephew Andrew's birthday.

When Benjamin and I returned home from my mother's at the end of the summer, the house felt empty and uncomfortably lonely. I anticipated my own bed bringing that glad-to-be-home sense of relief, but when my head hit the pillow at night, I could hear my doubts creaking up the wooden stairs. I slept with the television on, loudly redirecting my thoughts. With roughly six more weeks until John came back and three months until we welcomed our new son, there was a lot to accomplish in order to fill our house with the presence of home.

I started worrying about how the baby would affect Benjamin's life. How would I get Benjamin ready for school if the baby needed to eat? How would I get Benjamin to bed on time? He needed me to rock him to sleep every night. He'd lost his sucking reflex but was an avid pacifier lover, so I held it in place for him until he fell asleep. Benjamin still startled at any sudden loud noise. Would the baby's cries scare him? I tried to believe that we would learn to deal, like all families do, but everything that was going to potentially alter Benjamin's comfort and happiness brought on a renewed sense of guilt. What about the baby? Could I possibly love another child as much?

The list of nagging tasks included moving Benjamin into the master bedroom, packing away his Winnie the Pooh decorations, and creating a theme-less nursery for the baby. John and I would move into the old "therapy room." I wanted everything to be in place, to have a sense of organization. I wanted our home to look ready even if I wasn't.

When I first started dating John, I couldn't help but marvel at how neat his mother's home was, how everything was properly placed. I grew up in a clean but cluttered home littered with piles of magazines, bills, and random scraps of paper my mother had used to scribble out her grocery lists, monthly costs, and income. Our respective childhood homes perfectly reflected our families' dynamics. In my family, we discussed anything and everything. We fought unencumbered, slamming doors, and punching walls until we'd exhausted our problems and bodies. John's family was nonconfrontational. His father, an emphysema sufferer, spent most of his day alone in a bedroom he no longer shared with his wife. An uncomfortable silence existed between John's parents, but their home was picture-perfect.

I'm the type of person who needs to keep things out in the open so I don't forget about them. Over the years, John's need for order inspired me to minimize my clutter. Our home was well organized and the envy of all my friends. They saw a place of sanctity with wooden pillars, wainscoting, plaster ceiling medallions, Victorian light fixtures, artwork hanging from picture frame molding, and a stained-glass skylight hovering high above the center staircase. They marveled at toys stored in their bins without missing pieces and books neatly placed on shelves. They looked past Benjamin's gait trainer, stander, and specialized feeding chair because everything was thoughtfully placed. On most days, our tidy home gave me an illusion of peace to our otherwise emotionally chaotic lives. Sometimes I'd look around and see nothing but a mask of lies.

As a special educator, I analyze behaviors. I have long held the belief that behaviors are just a form of communication in the same way dance uses movement as a form of expression. In order to understand why a behavior exists, you need to identify the root cause and acknowledge when underlying causes aren't resolvable. My friends didn't see a problem with a tidy house or the anxious nesting desires of an expectant mother, but I knew my anxieties had less to do with shifting furniture and unpacking baby clothes and more with my failing efforts to beautify reality.

Benjamin had recently been through a repeat inpatient EEG, and we were experimenting with a new antiseizure medication cocktail. His seizures had become more frequent. They weren't the dreaded infantile spasms. These myoclonic seizures came in shorter clusters and were more predictable. Five minutes after flashing a wide morning smile, the electric storm began with a full body jolt, his arms thrusting forward and a quick deep gasp, followed by his pitiful cries. I'll never understand how he woke up happy. Didn't he remember from one morning to the next what was about to happen? He either lacked the capacity or was far more optimistic than I'll ever be. Every day I'd open his door, knowing I was about to set off a reaction I couldn't save him from. Even with a new baby on the way, I feared my feelings about motherhood would never change.

Twenty-one days before John was due back, I headed to the fetal brain specialist for another sonogram. During my first 3-D scan, I was excited to see my new son's face, to give him a clear identity. His tiny hands covered most of his face for the entire scan. It looked intentional, like he was trying to shield himself from the sun. I marveled at his fingers and the faintest hint of his nose, but his eyes remained covered. I couldn't formulate a complete picture without seeing his eyes.

I allowed my mind to be silent. At thirty weeks pregnant, I knew the doctor could assess the cortex of the brain. I stared at the small black-and-white screen. I waited for the doctor to speak, to break the silence, to fill the void that Benjamin's disability had blown into my life. Pointing to my son's brain, he said,

"There is just the right amount of gyri, no more, no less than expected. This baby does not have PMG." I held my tears with a slow, steady exhalation. *Thank you, God.*

The doctor suggested a fetal MRI to get a more detailed look at my son's brain. I couldn't stand the thought of my unborn child in an MRI machine. My memories of Benjamin in that tunnel were vivid enough to know I didn't want to crawl back into that hole. I'd heard what I needed to hear. As soon as I got out of there, I called John.

"The baby is fine. He does not have PMG!"

"That's such a relief. I mean I love Benjamin, but . . ."

"I know. I feel the same. We're always going to love Benjamin."

"Kiss him for me."

I rocked my firstborn son to sleep that night with a promise of eternal love. Our second son was free from his brother's fate, but I still felt the nagging need to remain guarded.

I lived by my calendar, crossing off the days until John would fly home, like a child pining for Christmas. A storm surrounding the Charleston area delayed his arrival. Having to wait even one more day was cruel. It felt like no matter how close I was to getting what I wanted in life, something always seemed to block me. We had only seven weeks left to organize. It's funny how my concept of time had shifted.

John neatly crafted a list of things to accomplish. We shopped for Benjamin's new bedroom furniture complete with a queen-size bed so we could easily cuddle with him. Two weeks into our preparations, at thirty-five weeks, I detected a brief dance of lights in front of my eyes. I called my neighbor, a doctor, and asked if he would come over and confirm that I had high blood pressure. During my pregnancy with Benjamin, I developed high blood pressure at thirty-six weeks and spent the next month in bed. It didn't surprise me when, once again, my doctor ordered bed rest, putting an abrupt halt to my nesting schedule. Dr.

Patrick planned to induce delivery, in two weeks, on November 11th. I was disappointed that the baby would definitely not share my nephew's birthday, but it was out of my control.

Benjamin must have sensed this hyperfocus on the baby and decided to see if he could pull rank and command our attention. He woke us in the middle of the night, screaming in a fashion we'd never heard before. I raced to his crib and found his mouth and face covered in blood. I frantically examined him to determine the origin of the bleeding. It was his hand. Somehow, he'd managed to bring his hand up to his mouth and bite into several fingers. He didn't have the ability to remove them in time.

That image of my unborn son peacefully sucking his thumb came back to me. Comparisons were a forbidden fruit, and I had miserably failed to resist its temptation. Motherhood was never going to be what I hoped for. Instead of having the freedom to encourage Benjamin to voluntarily bring his hands to his mouth, we were compelled to keep him safe. We bought special splints to keep his arms straight while he slept. It was one more piece of equipment to manage. He had daytime splints to keep his hands open, and foot orthotics to keep his feet and ankles properly aligned. My guilt barometer was set to worst mommy on the planet.

My fears mounted when Dr. Patrick detected the baby had an irregular heartbeat. Even though the subsequent fetal echocardiogram was normal, I had hit the point of emotional mayhem. I was in full-fledged worry mode despite all the previous testing. Four years of using defense mechanisms in order to get out of bed every morning had helped me build a well-layered wall of denial. I refused to think about labor, the massive life changes, and the quivering movements the baby was making. They reminded me of the shaking sensations I had during my pregnancy with Benjamin. I often wondered if he had seizures in utero. I pushed it all out of my head and embraced the reality that soon I would no longer be pregnant and would finally get to meet my new little boy. I concentrated on picking a name and welcoming something positive into our lives. I vowed that this would be the last baby. The stress was too great.

On the evening of November 3rd, I went to bed thinking that if the baby took after my side of the family, he'd be born the next day. November 4th is my brother John's birthday. I closed my eyes to the anxiety I was filled with every time I looked at Benjamin's bitten, bruised, and now infected fingers, and delighted in the humor of having a son swipe the bragging rights to my brother's birthdate. After all, I had to share my birthday with his son Evan.

At three fifteen in the morning, my water broke. I changed my clothes and lay back down, convinced I had just uncharacteristically wet the bed. A few minutes later, I wet myself again. Clinging to my denial, I searched my pregnancy books for a description of one's water breaking. Fifteen minutes later, I woke John and called the doctor, but I still thought it was a false alarm. I wasn't in pain.

Even though I wasn't having any contractions, I was in fact having the baby on my brother's birthday. The labor was considered preterm at thirty-six weeks, but Dr. Patrick didn't seem concerned and refused to preemptively call for a special pediatric team when we arrived at the hospital. Pitocin was started.

When I was pregnant with Benjamin, the doctor had induced labor with Pitocin. After all the books I read about the stages of labor, I'd expected a gradual progression of pain. As an ex-dancer and avid mover, I imagined I would avoid the confines of a hospital bed, walk around, crave massages, connect with my body, and embrace the physical process of birth. My Pitocin labor did not offer this textbook progression. My contractions were frequent and intense. While I'd impressed the OB-GYN on call with my ability to use my breath, as I had learned in dance and yoga, to labor unmedicated for five hours, I had no desire to get out of bed. During every painful wave, I'd close my eyes, unable to speak. If John so much as touched my arm in the middle of a contraction, I smacked him. If he offered a comforting word of encouragement, I'd wave him off. When an anesthesiologist stopped by to say hello, I lost all desire to have an unmedicated birth.

This time around, I wanted to avoid an epidural. I read about the Bradley Method because it offered a more thorough investigation of the physical and psychological process of birth. It appealed to my dancer mentality of managing pain and injury with massage, chiropractic, and physical therapy. I wanted to use the Bradley information as a guide, not a rulebook. After all, it is known as "Husband-Coached Childbirth," and although John was not a passive, queasy, sit-outside-in-the-hallway-and-call-me-when-it's-over kind of husband, I did not expect him to sit behind me, as pictured in the Bradley book, bare chested, actively guiding me through the birth of our son.

I had a different vision of the teamwork required for childbirth. I saw labor as something between my brain, my body, and the baby. I thought of John as my advocate, an objective observer, my friend, the person I love and trust with my life, who understands my actions, my silence, and my needs better than anyone. John is the type of husband who comes home at two in the morning and carries the laundry down to the basement, sets up my teacup and spoon for breakfast, and prepares Benjamin's daily medicine. He's the neighbor who cleans up trash on the street on his way to the grocery store and shovels other people's sidewalks.

When the Pitocin hit my bloodstream, and the contractions, once again, went from zero to fast and furious before John could dig out and wet the washcloth I'd packed, all I wanted to do was shut out the world. I couldn't handle one more piece of sensory input. I reminded John about my behavior during my labor with Ben. "Don't speak or touch me whenever I close my eyes." My mother, half deaf and sitting by the window, didn't get that message. During each contraction, I tried to direct my breath and clear my mind. For a time, I marveled at the way my muscles tightened sequentially from the top to the bottom of my uterus, just as the Bradley book described. I wanted to get out of my body's way, but my mother's voice brought me right back to reality. "Are you having a contraction now?"

Through clenched teeth I managed a "Yeeeeees." I love my mother. I wanted her there. It was supposed to be a day of bonding, but at that moment, I wanted nothing to do with her. The poor thing was already keeping her distance. It was hard for her to see me in any discomfort. Despite my best efforts to channel my inner dancer who never feared communicating with her body, I begged for an epidural as soon as my nurse mentioned the anesthesiologist. I was done managing my pain.

John and I passed the time by reading through two different baby name books. Although John thought the final decision should be mine because I was the one giving birth, I thought he should at least weigh in on the options. We wrote up a new short list: Zachary, Sebastian, and Jacob. John suggested, "How about Jim, in honor of your dance teacher?" Jim was a soft-spoken, reflective man. I can still imagine his long, lean form sauntering through Hunter's halls with his soft, blond curls and wire-framed eyeglasses. He'd greet everyone with a ready smile and southern Mississippi accent, "Hey, darlin'." I added his name to my list, knowing, as with Benjamin, that my unborn child's face would lead me to my decision.

Five hours after induction, I was ready to deliver. I hoped for a fast pushing stage. Benjamin had tested my every faculty. At one point, he appeared to be stuck. The OB, assuming his head was too large, performed an episiotomy. She looked up from between my legs, in horror, when I yelled, "Hey, hey, hey! I can feel that!" I later read that babies with CP are difficult to deliver because they lack the ability to move properly through the birth canal. Without my dance and gymnastics training, I doubt I would have been able to deliver him after just one hour of pushing.

Second babies are typically easier to deliver. After one effort, Dr. Patrick looked into my eyes and said, "Don't be afraid to push." A frantic voice repeated her words inside my head. *Don't be afraid to push. Really? I think I have every reason to be petrified. Those are the words you chose? Yes, and you know she's right. It's time.*

Nature is pretty incredible. Once that baby is out, the pain is done. We suffer for the cause of life. I reached for my son, ready to connect while John cut the cord. As I held him for the first time, the world seemed silent until I heard Dr. Patrick say, "You never see that." She and a medical student were staring between my legs. My blissful birth moment was suspended.

"What don't you ever see?"

"The cord is falling out by itself." It seemed that my son and I were in perfect sync. He wanted out early, and my body was so done being pregnant that it took care of the final stage of delivery without my knowledge or effort.

I love newborns. The feel of a baby lying on my torso and the way something so small can deliver so much renewed energy. His heartbeat against mine, giving each of my next breaths a focus and direction. I love being able to comfort with a touch, a kiss, or a song. My mother marveled at how simple the process appeared to be. Watching her cradle her ninth grandchild, I was suddenly inclined to agree.

He was, as Dr. Patrick said, "a respectable five pounds, five ounces, nineteen inches long." His Apgar scores were nine and nine, the same as Benjamin's. His head size was thirty-two centimeters, the same as Benjamin's, but he had a perfectly shaped head. Benjamin's appeared slightly narrow above his temples. This baby reminded me of the little boy in *Harold and the Purple*

Crayon. I ran a loop of names as I stared at his perfect little face. The only name that rang true was Sebastian. It was a big name for a little boy to grow into. The nurse said, "Sebastian sounds like the name of someone bound to do important things." I certainly hoped that would be the case. As if the name alone could guide his destiny.

A staff pediatrician arrived to do the standard newborn examination. The delivery room was small, and the infant isolate was just a little more than an arm's reach away. The doctor turned Sebastian to look at his back, and I caught a glimpse of what looked like a second anal opening. Now that was something I didn't expect to see. "What the hell is that?"

He laughed and, without hesitation, reassured me, "You only have to worry if you hear me say that. It's called a sacral dimple, an indentation in the skin along the spine. It's common and is usually nothing to worry about. It appears to be completely sealed. You can have a scan done to rule out any underlying spinal defect if your pediatrician has any concerns." I relaxed.

The nurse took blood to check Sebastian's glucose level. It seemed low. They checked it again. It was low. I tried to give him glucose water, but he had just finished breastfeeding and was completely uninterested. "Why don't you . . ." my mother began, but I cut her off. The contractions were over, but there was a new wave of irritation building. Confined to the table, my legs still unreliable from the epidural, a completely unrelated numbness began to spread.

The doctor's demeanor grew serious. "Tell me again about your other son's condition." I detailed Benjamin's medical history. "Okay, now I am a bit concerned." He stepped out of the room.

Sebastian continued to refuse a bottle, and I pushed myself to retain control while my mind tossed the facts: early delivery, sacral dimple, low glucose, and a bluish patch on his backside called a Mongolian spot. What did it mean? The doctor returned with an answer. The staff had used the wrong glucose meter. His level was fine.

For the next two days, John and I enjoyed time alone with Sebastian. We fell into a more carefree mood, very reminiscent of our first week with Benjamin. John teased, "Sebastian, your legs are so skinny."

I added, "You'd be rejected on a turkey farm."

Compared to newborn Benjamin's seven pounds, fourteen ounces, Sebastian was petite, but he was eating well. A nurse stopped by. "Do you have the breast pump in here?"

"No, we don't need it. He's eating just fine."

"Well, he's the only baby on the floor who is."

"Looks like you're the best-behaved child on the unit, Sebastian!"

The next evening, another nurse peeked in. "You aren't first-time parents, are you?"

"No, we have an almost-four-year-old at home."

"I could tell. There's a real calm in this room."

To help us maintain that sense of peace, Benjamin's neurologist stopped by to give Sebastian a quick exam. I cringed as he placed a measuring tape around Sebastian's head. "Everything looks normal." As he lifted Sebastian up to his shoulder, I heard the voice of my silent whisperer: *Was it normal the way Sebastian just hyperextended his head?*

"He's a strong baby." Dr. Gold smiled.

I reached for Sebastian, certain of only one thing. I wasn't finished worrying about head size or my own personal growth.

8

The Body Is an Orchestra
of Individual Voices

A time to keep silence, and a time to speak

When Sebastian was two weeks old, I dubbed him "Mr. Shifty Eyes." I would nurse him, longing to lock into a steady gaze. Sebastian didn't look at me with the same intensity Benjamin had. As a special educator, I focused on even the smallest soft signs. Soft signs are behaviors that are just slightly off the norm. They aren't obvious like a seizure. They are hardly-worth-mentioning behaviors that for some kids mean absolutely nothing, but in others mean everything, like inconsistent eye contact.

Sebastian's lack of focus bothered me enough to discuss it with Benjamin's physical therapist. She said her newborn niece was exhibiting the very same behavior, so I told myself I couldn't use Benjamin's development as any kind of guideline for Sebastian. Of course Benjamin stared at me. He didn't have the physical capacity to do much else while I nursed him. Sebastian had freedom of movement and a curiosity about the world Benjamin lacked.

Life with two children was hectic but glorious, as otherwise insignificant newborn norms lulled me. We would wrap Sebastian in a blanket, burrito-style, and stand aside as he squirmed and wiggled in order to break out of the blanket. He'd conclude this dance by removing his little knit hat. I never grew tired of watching him do this. It was as if I could feel him stripping away the layers of my fears.

Benjamin found his voice as a big brother. Every time Sebastian cried, instead of being startled, Benjamin screeched with delight. Perhaps it was his way of teasing his brother, or maybe he thought the joke was on us.

Wanting to cultivate a more positive state of mind, I decided to unsubscribe from the Internet lissencephaly support group. It was a difficult but necessary choice. I had a healthy newborn, and I just couldn't manage mourning the loss of even one more child. I needed to cut the line that had me binding Benjamin to all this grief. I wanted to celebrate life. There had been enough pain in my heart. It was time for unobstructed love.

When Sebastian was about a month old, we discovered a lump under the skin in between his eyes. I joked that it was actually a horn. Like Benjamin, Sebastian was a happy, non-colicky baby. When I looked into his eyes, I saw more than a curious child. I sensed a wild inner drive. John's brother Mario, known for nicknaming every infant family member, dubbed Sebastian "The Maniac Man."

Dr. Gabriel referred us to a neurosurgeon because the mass was in the midline of his face. The neurosurgeon explained that the lesion was either superficial or there could be an intracranial extension. If the latter were true, he would need a surgery where they would cut the top of his head from ear to ear. The thought of having Sebastian's head peeled open like an orange in order to remove a cyst was more than a little disturbing.

At that time, Benjamin was recovering from his first surgery to lengthen several of the tendons in his lower extremities. His muscles had tightened so much that he wasn't able to straighten out his legs anymore. I felt like a Ping-Pong ball racing from one child's needs to another, getting smacked at every turn. I was, however, grateful that no matter what the diagnosis was for Sebastian, at least it was something the doctors could fix.

At six months old, Sebastian had his turn in an MRI machine. Some families have a collection of baby portraits. I have brain scans. Sebastian's lump was a superficial dermoid cyst. With the threat of brain surgery behind us, we prepared for our first summer as a family of four. John headed off to work on location, this time in Canada. I was not about to spend another summer separated from John, especially with our tenth wedding anniversary coming up in August. Once Benjamin was finished with summer school, I would take the boys to Canada.

Traveling by plane with two children, especially one who is physically disabled, was not exactly a relaxing way to start a getaway. Even with my talent for choreography and my mother along for support, the task of maneuvering an eight-month-old, a four-and-a-half-year-old, a car seat, and an oversized adaptive stroller was more than challenging. Connecting flights and Benjamin crying from the moment of takeoff made for a long trip. Note to self: Never take another family vacation that requires air travel unless I am heavily medicated.

The rest of the trip was surprisingly enjoyable. I didn't know what to expect from the extremely flat plains in the middle of Canada, but Winnipeg was quite kid-friendly. With a rented house out of the main section of the city, we got a taste of the quiet, suburban life. As much as I loved Brooklyn and our house, I had to admit a detached home with an attached double garage made life with two children and all their equipment a lot easier. I could live without searching for parking spots and schlepping sleepy kids for blocks.

While John worked, I bathed in the joy of watching Sebastian crawl, sit, stand, and climb. He explored every park, beach, pool, and outdoor summer festival with curiosity and that mischievous look in his eyes. All was right with the world.

In the fall of 2003, I went back to my early intervention work and looked forward to Sebastian's first birthday. We planned a kiddie gym party at the dance studio where I used to work. It was wonderful to have my son among a room full of active toddlers. I finally felt comfortable with other mothers and their children. Sebastian took his first steps and could sustain an interest in a variety of toys for an impressive amount of time. He easily entertained himself. His first word approximations emerged: "Mama, Dada, stop, cat, ball, up." For the next several months, our days were busy with music and gym classes.

In the spring, Benjamin was rounding out his final year in preschool. A climate of dread surrounds parents whose children are aging out of preschool. In our minds, early intervention is homey, preschool provides a safe haven, but kindergarten places a true separation between the school and the parents. This is true for all kindergarteners, but Benjamin was not like most five-year-olds, and I didn't like the thought of having even less control and access to his day-to-day experiences.

In addition to transition stress, we were preparing Benjamin for his seventh hospital stay for a second tendon-lengthening surgery. The first surgery, to straighten out his legs, had been successful beyond our expectations. We hoped to see a similar outcome on his arms, but he's a fighter. As soon as the casts came off, he flexed both arms tight.

The tension in our lives increased when John and I took Sebastian for his standard eighteen-month checkup. I shared a growing concern with Dr. Gabriel: "Sebastian hasn't gained any new words since his first birthday."

He shook his head. "Give him a little more time. Boys are often late talkers, and he doesn't have a sibling who can model for him."

I got the feeling Dr. Gabriel did not want to entertain the thought of our family having any more problems with child development. Looking at John, I shrugged. "Okay, we'll wait." I fought to crush the sprouting of my old frightful garden of doubt. I relieved myself of those new anxieties by refocusing on the crops over on the Benjamin side of my brain.

Sitting across from our school district's Kindergarten Turning Five team, on the parents' side of the table, I was ready to do battle if they cut down Benjamin's therapeutic services. As a teacher, I'd witnessed some sly Grinch-like administrators. After months of preparation, I was ready to fight, but the team offered services that surpassed his preschool mandates. Off the record, because they were only responsible for determining eligibility, they also told me about a school on Staten Island that would be perfect for Benjamin. When John and I first bought our house, we viewed it as a tremendous compromise because Bay Ridge was much farther from Manhattan than our apartment in Brooklyn Heights. Now Bay Ridge's close proximity to Staten Island made our decision worthwhile. Door to door, the commute to the Staten Island school was thirty minutes.

Because he was classified as having "multiple disabilities," the Board of Education's specialized citywide District 75 would make Benjamin's actual school placement. As I expected, District 75 offered a Brooklyn placement. When I toured the school, I was shocked to see that some of Benjamin's old preschool classmates seemed disengaged, lacking their once vibrant personalities. Knowing such a subjective observation wouldn't matter, I declined the placement based on the school's inability to meet Benjamin's loaded therapy mandates. The District 75 placement office denied my request for the Staten Island program twice. Benjamin was nothing more than an ID number to a bunch of strangers sitting in their Manhattan offices.

By July, John and I were considering moving upstate where

we'd toured a private school recommended by Benjamin's physical therapist. We justified a move to the suburbs with the need to find a ranch-style house, but there was no guarantee the local upstate school district would agree to send Benjamin to the school we wanted, and we weren't ready to leave Brooklyn anyway. I'd stay up late at night strategizing the next move against the Board of Ed, and when John would come home at two in the morning, we'd discuss the options. One night, in what my sports-loving husband would refer to as a Hail Mary pass, I suggested, "I have the number of a District 75 placement officer that a parent and a secretary at the local district office gave me. Maybe this guy will listen to us."

John said, "Call him."

"No. You call him. The last thing this guy needs is to hear from another screaming mommy."

One phone call from John secured Benjamin's placement. The placement officer explained to him that the two previous denials were based on the BOE's reluctance, in our post-9/11 world, to transport Benjamin over the Verrazzano-Narrows Bridge—a flimsy excuse since our neighbor's child was already making that same commute. So I learned the importance of delegating jobs to my husband. When my mommy friends are nervous about their children's IEP meetings, I tell them, "You have to bring penis to the table, especially when dick is on the other side."

It took a month for the BOE to hire a nurse to ride the bus with Benjamin. He needed to travel with rectal Valium in case of prolonged seizures. Fortunately, John was between jobs, so we drove Benjamin back and forth every day. One morning on the way to school, Sebastian's continued language delays dominated our conversation. John stared at the road as he drove. "I think we need to tell Dr. Gabriel that something's not right."

"John, he's such a physically active boy. It's not uncommon."

He glanced at me. "He's twenty-two months old, and he's not speaking. He's not even using the six words he had."

I threw my hands in the air. "Why do you always have to be so pessimistic?"

He stared at me hard. Then he turned to Sebastian and yelled, "Sebastian . . . Sebastian . . . Sebastian!"

Silence.

Sebastian stared out the window without a trace of response.

John shook his head and pointed at Sebastian. "That's not normal."

John had an objectivity I didn't want to appreciate. While he always had a tight bond with Benjamin, he hadn't formed a significant connection with Sebastian. I made excuses. After all, he'd missed months of Sebastian's first year while on location. When he was working locally, he only saw the boys on the weekends. It would be ridiculous for him to expect to have the same kind of bond I enjoyed with Sebastian. Plus, I nursed Sebastian for fourteen months. I put in the time to bond. John hadn't. John didn't buy my rationalizations. Years later, he would confess that when we first arrived in Canada, he took one look at Sebastian and saw a wide-eyed baby who didn't seem to recognize his own father and thought, *Something's wrong with him.*

While we continued the drive to Benjamin's school, the special educator part of my brain knew John was right, but the parent part of me quickly worked to create a force field around the words that suddenly hung in the space between my young son and my heart. I couldn't do it again. I couldn't have another child who was disabled. Nope. Not again. *It's just a speech delay. We can take care of it with speech therapy.* I stomped hard on the roots of terror thrusting at the soles of my feet.

Sebastian's behavior was reminiscent of my niece Caitlin's, diagnosed as a toddler with pervasive developmental disorder not otherwise specified. PDD-NOS sounded like a generic term doctors used when they couldn't quite put their finger on a more accurate diagnosis, but it was code for *We think your child's autistic, but she's not affected severely enough to say she's autistic.* Ten years before I had Sebastian, I had been fascinated by Caitlin's ability to ignore me as I clapped my hands directly behind her head. As a supplement to her preschool education, Caitlin took one of my gymnastics classes. Teaching her and other children with autism at the dance studio led me to my graduate studies in special education after I left dance.

Sebastian is not Caitlin, I told myself over and over. It was true that he didn't always respond to his name, but he didn't ignore me. He played appropriately with toys. Boys, especially very active boys, often lag in language abilities. I was settling into this foggy, subjective view of Sebastian's delays when I ran into a special educator friend in a local playground.

Claire had a son who was exactly the same age as Sebastian. We hadn't seen each other for a while. As the boys ran around, I looked to her for some reassurance. "It can be normal for kids to drop vocabulary, right? I mean, couldn't Sebastian just be following some slower yet typical developmental path?"

Before she could answer, her son ran over talking nonstop. According to developmental charts, two-year-olds speak in two-to-four-word sentences. Not this boy. When and how had he gotten so verbal? As soon as he left, I threw my hands up. "I don't know what else to do for Sebastian. I talk to him, read to him, and sing to him every day. How hard do I have to work to teach him how to talk?"

She looked at me and said, "You don't."

Another miserable moment of truth. I had become so accustomed to working one hundred times harder to help my sons accomplish the most minor tasks. I allowed myself to believe children needed everything taught directly to them. It's just not the case.

In order to raise my children, I'd divided myself into battling parent and teacher parts. The Limón technique taught me that the body is like an orchestra, made up of different instrumental voices. The individual voices (body parts) can work together, but in order to demonstrate clarity, you have to choose which body part is leading the movement. This first isolated body part sequentially leads the next body part into motion. In dance, it's easy to see unnatural choices. As the great modern dance pioneer Martha Graham said, "Movement never lies." In the world of parenting children with disabilities, there isn't always an obvious sequence to follow.

I sedated the mother's voice inside me and looked at my son with a clinician's eye. I started with two major goals. First, I had to teach Sebastian how to point. Most toddlers use their determined little pointer fingers to draw your attention to things they want to learn about and share with you. They point to the sky to show a bird or point to the cabinet to ask for a cookie. Sebastian had other nonverbal strategies, and with my ability to analyze movement and behavior, I could meet his needs, but I knew the lack of pointing was a major red flag. I took Polaroid pictures of Sebastian's favorite foods and grouped them by categories: breakfast, lunch, dinner, and snacks. I created a board with Velcro strips and placed the appropriate options on the board throughout the day. I would give him what he wanted only when he pointed to a picture. It was a modified version of a program used by speech therapists. Sebastian learned how to use the board in one week.

The second goal was to elicit any form of purposeful verbal communication. When he woke in the morning, I would open his door, make eye contact, and then close the door. I would sit outside his room to see if he would call out. At first, he just went back to playing on his own, so I'd knock on the door. I'd call him and wait for any vocalization. When it came, I would walk in and praise him. I would sit on the floor encouraging and waiting again for a second vocalization before I would lift him out of the crib. Special educators call this task analysis. You take a specific goal and break it down into several small sequential steps.

I made a request for early intervention services and hired one of Benjamin's preschool speech therapists to work privately with Sebastian at home. My lovely little wild child wasn't thrilled. While Benjamin was smitten with his pretty professional ladies, Sebastian wanted to run away. In order to contain him, I used one of Benjamin's therapeutic chairs complete with a seat belt and locking tray. Although I was afraid it would incite him, the chair calmed him down, and he focused on the lessons. He was the one locked in the chair, but I felt like the prisoner.

I had been considering a third child. When I broached the subject with John, he said, "I thought we were done, but I'm willing to discuss it." Consumed with the guilt that Sebastian would in his lifetime bury his mother, father, and only brother, I didn't want him to be alone in the world. I read memoirs of siblings of children with disabilities. But now, with Sebastian's development in question, John and I agreed another pregnancy was absolutely not an option.

December 2004. Early intervention initial evaluation, take two was like the movie *Groundhog Day* with a twist. It might have been a different son and new evaluators, but that awful no-good feeling in the pit of my stomach was completely reminiscent. We only had one week of unadulterated joy after Benjamin was born. I suppose I should have been grateful that with Sebastian we had more than a year of experiencing the truer joys of parenthood, but I was too busy hanging streamers for my pity party.

I brought Sebastian to Benjamin's old preschool for his arena-style assessment. There was some comfort in familiarity, but my breakfast club moms were nowhere in sight. Although they were all just a phone call away, I was alone again, the only parent with two children with disabilities. As a parent and educator, I

Fall *and* Recovery

find evaluations my least favorite part of the process. They represent a snapshot of the child. Like all pictures, they can only capture what you are capable of seeing. Test kits and developmental standards set the perimeters. The results seem so rigid and unforgiving. I awaited the barrage of questions regarding every aspect of Sebastian's development since birth.

No tears this time. I was in clinician mode, subduing my parental woes and wearing my informant's hat. We were in a small office with the social worker, special educator, and speech therapist. Sebastian was in a hyperactive mood, hopping, dancing, spinning, climbing on and jumping off chairs. It was like watching an adorable, caged animal on display at a carnival show. Once again, I provided the needed history, watched my son's behavior, and made predictions about what their perceptions would be.

The parent voice within me resisted my teacher logic. Perhaps Sebastian's high level of physical activity had something to do with his language delays. It was as if he learned to walk one day, and then the next he began to prance. I could just about see Sebastian's motor running. I looked to the speech evaluator. "I have a nephew who has attention-deficit/hyperactivity disorder. Could that be a consideration?"

She shook her head. "It's unlikely that hyperactivity would deter the language skills of a child who is read to every single day."

Another evaluator commented, "Does he always climb on furniture? It's indicative of poor safety awareness."

I've seen "poor safety awareness" on countless autism workshop handouts. I shifted in my seat. "No, he doesn't do that at home." It's relevant to note poor safety awareness if a child is prone to running into the street without looking for cars, but if Sebastian could physically climb and jump, why would he or I perceive the activity as dangerous? He'd been navigating a variety of climbing structures in his gym class. I'm pretty sure I was climbing furniture well after the age of two. I used my parents' bed as a trampoline and didn't think twice about tumbling on concrete. Sebastian never attempted anything he couldn't actually do.

I didn't admit it to the team, but some of Sebastian's movements made no sense. He'd stop mid-activity and break into a hopping routine. It seemed purposeful to him. He appeared to be in control, but there was no consistency as to frequency or duration. I was tired of placing every one of my son's behaviors under the microscope. If you look close enough at anyone, you'll find problems.

When the evaluation report packet arrived in the mail, I hesitated to open it. When I write any report, I am sure to debrief the parents before they see it. Obviously, they vary from writer to writer, but there are basic similarities. Their sole purpose is to report developmental findings and to justify or exclude the need for services. First, they give a standard social history provided by the parents. Next comes some perfunctory positive character observation—Yes, I know my son has adorable curly brown hair. Then, based on the assessment tool used, they plunge into a litany of age-appropriate skills that your child can and cannot perform. Six developmental domains are tested:

- Gross motor, covering large muscle groups
- Fine motor, including small muscle groups and sensory integration, the ability to manage information gathered from one's senses
- Cognitive, pertaining to information processing
- Speech/language, relating to the ability to understand language and express oneself
- Social/emotional, referring to play skills and the ability to interact with others
- Self-help skills, consisting of daily living activities

At that time, in order to qualify for services a child had to show a 33 percent delay in one area or a 25 percent delay in two or more areas. Sebastian's reports disclosed that he had qualifying delays in the areas of cognition, communication, social/emotional, and self-help. Each deficit jumped off the page and danced inside my mind. The ingredients were blending, and I watched as my fears expanded like a soufflé.

When you have a child with disabilities, evaluations fall under the category of read it once, can't digest it, hide it in a file, and don't look at it again until you are sure you will not be operating heavy machinery. It might be appropriate if the large manila packet came with an FDA-type warning label that states: *Do not read this if you are already in a bad mood. Do not read this if you're having the best day of your life. Do not read this near an open window if you live above the first floor. Do not plan on submerging yourself in water, rummaging through your medicine cabinet, buying a gun, cooking with knives, using your oven, and by all means, do not read this if you are expected to function rationally anytime in the near future.*

I was in full-fledged hang-some-streamers, inflate-balloons, and set-out-appetizers feeling-sorry-for-myself mode. I stared at the recommendations for speech and special education services and all the neatly detailed percentages of delays. The voice of my OB-GYN rushed to my forebrain: "Lightning never strikes twice." In my world it had. The forceful jagged dagger marked my center. Angry that I dared to stand back up the first time, it bore a dark tunnel through the surface of the earth. With all its might, it dragged me down and scorched me layer by layer. The deeper I went within myself, the more I prayed for death.

My sister-in-law suggested that I ask my doctor for some kind of medication. Maybe my pain was too difficult for her to witness, but I had zero interest in artificial relief. The significance of being present and fully attending to the moment is not exclusive to positive experiences. I had tried to tune in to the version of motherhood everyone else had, but my radio played a deafening static. I wanted to feel every miserable sensation. Pain was the messenger sent to remind me that I was still very much alive.

I treated each day like a checklist of basic tasks that needed to be performed: get out of bed, shower, dress, brush my teeth, take care of Benjamin and Sebastian, and go to work. Sebastian's disability, I decided, was my punishment for not baptizing him. John and I discussed it but decided to wait and expose Sebastian to religion in a more historical and educational context. He could make his own decisions about God and church. Hell, maybe God was angry that John and I didn't have a religious wedding ceremony. Like many of his friends, John's faith in God lapsed during childhood when science seemed to better explain the ways of the world. I believed in God but had long ago lost the need to equate faith with the formalities dictated by the church. When I was a teenager, my mother explained to a parish priest that she couldn't attend Sunday mass because she had to work. The priest said, "You don't have to come to church, just send your envelope."

Guilt and grief dominated my thoughts until I had a conversation with my stepbrother's wife, Rufina. She is twelve years my junior and a former dancer, raised with the traditions and superstitions of the Russian Jewish community. There is an endearing mystique about her. Rufina has a gift for seeing and acknowledging the good in others. She is the most genuine human being I know, but, in her early years of motherhood, she didn't trust her instincts and turned to me on many occasions for child-rearing advice.

On that day, she pulled me back to humanity. Moaning into the phone, I complained, "I don't deserve to suffer the fate of a mother with two children with disabilities."

In a sober yet supportive tone, she responded, "No one deserves it." It was just the cold drink in the face I needed. Pity party over. I wasn't the only mother on the planet having this experience. This was not a punishment. I had no idea how I was going to take care of two children with such dramatically different needs. I would have to go back to the basic lessons. One day at a time. Don't think too far ahead.

At Sebastian's Individualized Family Service Plan meeting, the district representative sat next to Sebastian. "Show me your nose."

Sebastian pointed to his nose.

"Good. Hum with me."

Sebastian's sweet little voice hummed "Twinkle, Twinkle, Little Star."

"Very good."

These were the compliant types of behaviors that so often allowed me to deny the truth. *Oh my Sebastian, I do wonder.* Always the tense stage mother, I was proud of my little performer. I thought I heard the evaluators releasing their collective breaths as well.

Afterward, the director of early intervention pulled me aside. I rarely saw Sylvia on her feet and out from behind her desk. She was an older woman with physical disabilities. Grabbing my arm and lowering her voice, she told me, "Sebastian did so well today. During the evaluation we were really worried." There was just something about her intonation that jarred me. In all the years Benjamin had gone to school there, I had never been the mom who everyone looked at with pity. Yet there it was now, coming from a woman with crooked fingers and a labored gait. It's one thing to feel as if life has beaten you up. It's quite another when you realize everyone is staring at your scars.

It was time to air out our wounds. Early intervention evaluations do not give a diagnosis, but I knew what the unspoken speculation was. John and I brought the boys for their annual checkups. We confronted Dr. Gabriel with the reality that Sebastian was, in our opinion, autistic. He didn't agree and, just to prove us wrong, referred us to a pediatric developmentalist at Mt. Sinai Hospital.

Sebastian was two and a half when we brought him in for the evaluation. The doctor asked if we would allow students to observe. We were used to teaching hospitals and made no objections. Beginning the lesson, the doctor gave Sebastian some toys. With an outstretched hand he asked Sebastian, "Give me the car."

No response.

The doctor touched the car while asking again, "Give me the car."

Sebastian held on tight to it with his eyes focused only on the car.

The doctor turned to the students. "That was a refusal and is not counted against him." As Sebastian continued to play, the doctor tried to draw his attention to a new toy. He didn't look at it or the doctor. When Sebastian ignored his request to share a play experience and failed to make eye contact, the doctor explained, "He's displaying a lack of joint attention." It must have taken him all of fifteen minutes to pronounce, "He has PDD-NOS." There it was: my niece Caitlin's diagnosis. He added, "Now they're calling it ASD—autism spectrum disorder." I guessed "they," the medical powers that be, decided not to hide autism behind the broad, generic PDD-NOS term, but calling autism a spectrum disorder didn't feel much more specific or comprehensible.

There was a short, tense moment in which I felt as though I'd missed my cue. The curtain was up, and I wasn't onstage yet. The doctor and his students seemed to await our reaction. I did as well. It wasn't like the day of Benjamin's diagnosis. There wasn't that shock factor. Still, it wasn't something we wanted to hear.

My gaze drifted from Sebastian to the doctor and then to John. There was a distinct lack of emotion among us all. The presence of the students allowed me to look at my son like a clinical subject. I felt like one too. I approached my mark. Instead of presenting like an injured parent, I put on my professional educator face and said, "At this stage we want your opinion about educational services. Sebastian is receiving speech and special education instruction at home."

The doctor said, "I have found that children like Sebastian tend to do very well with early intervention and are often mainstreamed into the general education classroom by kindergarten."

As we left, I gave John my interpretation. "Sounds like we have the right supports in place."

"Let's hope he's right about mainstreaming by kindergarten."

With nothing more to do, I called Dr. Gabriel and gave him the diagnosis.

"I don't believe it," he said. "This is the first time I'm going to disagree with him."

I thought his honorable emotional investment in our family caused him to turn to denial as a coping strategy.

I wanted to sit on that bench with him, but the stillness would only give me more time to realize that my two biggest fears as a parent had rippled their way into my pond. Multiply disabled and autistic, what were the odds? How were we going to live with two? I had given John two sons who would never share his passions. Although John was quiet, he wore his devastation and embodied the part with his black clothes and increasingly weighted gait. His hair, once a vibrant fluff of black curls, was now a thin, limp, dull gray collection.

My hair hadn't lost its chestnut-brown coloring. My gray was on the inside, slowly darkening my humor. *Well, Joanne, you have one child with half a brain and another who'll be out of his mind. At least if Benjamin does die, maybe Sebastian won't care.*

9

Stay at Home

A time to mourn, and a time to dance

I can still imagine the day we brought Sebastian home from
the hospital. I stood frozen at the top of our stoop. As John
placed the key in the front door, I stopped him. "Wait. Just give
Benjamin one more moment in the life he knows." I tried to visualize my sons' first introduction, but the weight of Sebastian in
his infant carrier distracted me. If I held him with two hands in
front of me, my back ached. When I switched the carrier to my
right hand, most of my weight shifted to my right foot. I struggled to find a comfortable counterbalance. *Joanne, just breathe and
stand on two feet.*

Standing on two feet was a directive I'd heard in dance class
many times, and something I often thought about in my pedestrian life, especially after the day I was waiting for the elevator at
Hunter with Jim and an eccentric classmate whom most people
avoided. The student turned to Jim and said, "I've been watching
her for a while. What do you think she needs to do to improve
her technique?" As I shook off a creepy stalked feeling, Jim
answered, "Right now, all she needs to do is stand on two feet."
Always the good student, I shifted my weight and appreciated
the feeling of groundedness.

The instant Benjamin met Sebastian, he was all smiles and laughter. Sebastian slept through the encounter. I sat back admiring John's features on my sons' faces and the new family circle we had formed. Now I missed that sense of calm connectedness. Nothing about lissencephaly, autism, or John's work schedule afforded me any balance.

For most of our married life, John has worked on big-budget, feature films. He still shrugs off the importance of his position as a production coordinator. "I'm like an office manager." From a wife's perspective, I disagree. While the big name studios have permanent offices and staff in Los Angeles, New York film crews are pieced together project to project. During preproduction, prior to actually shooting, John sets up the production office from scratch, ordering everything from furniture and phone lines to milk and coffee. The office needs to accommodate the director, producers, and multiple departments including art, props, special effects, and accounting, to name a few. John hires and supervises the assistant coordinator, production assistants, and secretaries. During those start-up days, John might get home by ten or eleven at night. When the film is shooting, the demands on the production office grow. If the director wants a special crane for an overhead shot, John has to order it. If the actors are traveling, need a hotel room, a cab, a specific brand of water in their trailer, or a revised script, it's up to the production office. If someone gets hurt on set, John's filling out the Workers' Comp forms. When I say John works eighteen hours a day, I'm not exaggerating. When the director calls a wrap on set, John is in the office waiting for the Directors Guild trainee to bring him information for the daily production reports. By the time he finishes filling out all the forms and prepping for the next day's shoot, he decides whether to drive home and catch three hours of sleep or stay in the office and get five.

As a department head, John holds himself responsible for the work of his entire staff. Even when he's home on the weekend, emails and phone calls pour in. I wish he'd delegate more, but he's a perfectionist. He's a phenomenal production coordinator, but there's no balance between work and family. When the office is open on the weekends, the boys and I can go weeks without seeing or speaking to John. If I'm lucky, he'll find time to send me a rushed email:

I hate my life
But not you
I love you
And the boys
You're the best!

I wasn't the best, but bothering John about the boys just wasn't an option. John's work habits had been well defined and unbreakable long before we had children. I never expected him to change, but in the earlier years of parenthood, I wasn't always good at playing the role of a single parent, especially raising two children with equally frustrating diagnoses.

Although autism was a well-known disability, its origin and prospects for remediation were as mysterious as Benjamin's very rare condition. Sebastian followed in his brother's educational footsteps. He started with home-based early intervention and then transitioned to the local, segregated, EI center-based program during the summer before his third birthday. Even though Sebastian was making progress, I wasn't convinced he should transition to a segregated preschool program in September.

It wasn't that Sebastian didn't have significant delays. His eye contact was inconsistent, he didn't always respond to his name, and he wasn't talking, but he had strengths. Whenever I hung out with the moms I'd met at Benjamin's preschool, they liked to point out all the seemingly normal things Sebastian was doing:

"Look at how well he plays with his train set."

"He loves to play chase."

"He loves books."

"He smiles at you."

"He points to all the food pictures to communicate what he wants."

Although I knew it broke a fundamental rule of parenting children with disabilities, my family compared Sebastian to my niece. Sebastian was more social, and Caitlin had been educated in inclusion classrooms. I had studied inclusion intensively in my graduate program. Inclusion extended the concept of normalization—the idea that everyone should be included in natural environments and that the community takes responsibility for those with greater needs—into the classroom.

In terms of educational placement, children with disabilities are supposed to be educated in the least restrictive environment, meaning as close to the general education class as possible alongside their nondisabled peers. The developmentalist had seemed very encouraging about inclusion classrooms. But could Sebastian thrive in an integrated environment? Would a segregated classroom be the better option? Would two years in either environment prepare him for kindergarten, or would he always be so far behind?

I was in a corridor staring at two identical blank doors. Which was right? Which was wrong? Was it that simple? Does one choice save a child from the grasp of autism? What if I picked the wrong key? Would his door ever open? What if the key broke in the door? What kind of educator was I if I couldn't even be certain about my own child's education? I ignored the advice I'd so often given parents: "Accept that there are no perfect answers. Do what you are capable of and stop judging yourself."

My performance training had taught me how to navigate unexpected problems. At Hunter, in the days before a concert, we'd move our rehearsals from the dance studio to the stage. The whole company would sit in the audience with the artistic director as she took performance notes. Full stage rehearsals included dancing with costumes, music, and lighting in order to reduce the risk of human error. What if the lights came up and the music didn't start, or a prop ended up in the wrong place onstage? Jana would remind us, "The audience doesn't know the choreography. They'll only notice a mistake if you show indecisiveness. Just stay focused and keep going. Make a choice and do it with commitment."

Most things aren't within a single dancer's power to control. Dancing with others requires flexibility. There is an expectation to perform specific movements at the exact right moment and place. If I botched a step, it could affect my next move and the people around me and disrupt the overall image and intent the choreographer was hoping to display. I felt a tremendous responsibility to my fellow dancers, the choreographer, and the audience. Everyone involved in a dance production wants to get it right. When things go wrong, you can't just freeze and let everyone stumble. Eventually, the curtain will come down, and the opportunity for fulfillment will be lost. There's no time to waste on personal angst. Sebastian's future was depending on me to make the right choice at the right moment. I was stumbling through this transition, and I knew it.

Typically, when parents are conflicted about placement options, I tell them, "Go look at different schools. You'll know the right one when you see it. You'll feel it in your gut." I decided to take my own advice, and even though it's stressful for John to take time off work, I asked him to make time. We started with a local private general education preschool. My friend Claire, whose chatty son helped me realize Sebastian was off the normal developmental course, told me the school was highly regarded for its concentration on social skills development. Children like Sebastian attended school with help from the Board of Education.

The BOE paid for a certified special education itinerant teacher (SEIT) to work one-to-one with a student and monitor their progress. We sat with the school director and her current SEIT as they observed Sebastian and reviewed his evaluations. Sebastian walked around the office touching every knickknack in sight. I gave John a look as if to say, "Focus on him so I can concentrate on this list of questions you put me in charge of."

"Sebastian was diagnosed with PDD-NOS, although we don't have that in writing. Have you worked with children on the spectrum?"

The SEIT said, "I've worked here for several years with children much more severe than Sebastian."

The director added, "We once had a child who started the school year hiding underneath chairs eating lint. He did very well. I don't see any reason why Sebastian shouldn't be given the chance to be in a general education classroom."

Next, John and I met with the educational supervisor at the segregated preschool affiliated with the early intervention program Sebastian was already attending. She showed us a class of twelve children who had various abilities. The class was similar to the EI class Sebastian was in, and I could see him thriving surrounded by peers who would serve as positive role models.

Then she suggested we look at a class of six children, one teacher, and two assistant teachers. As we climbed to the third floor, I could feel my blood pressure rising with each step. John had no idea we were about to witness a classroom designed for and typically limited to students with autism. It was even more restrictive than Benjamin's classroom. We walked into the rather small room. Most preschool classrooms display student artwork and posters of the alphabet, numbers, or shapes, but these walls were bare. It was purposefully devoid of external distractions. Partitions made even smaller private work areas. Some desks faced the walls inside closets.

The children sat in a semicircle in the middle of the room. The teacher pointed to the large calendar on the wall, singing about the days of the week. Then she asked, "What day is it today?" She looked at her students.

Silence.

She continued, "Today is Monday. Today is Monday."

I was standing slightly behind John, wanting to give him a let's-get-out-of-here look when one of the assistant teachers showed me a "discrete trial" binder filled with data collection sheets used to record the skills being worked on with the students.

I turned to the educational supervisor and said, "We're not looking for an ABA class." ABA—applied behavior analysis—is a widely recognized and sought-out treatment program used in educating children with autism.

She was quick to counter, "It isn't ABA."

Technically, she was right. I misspoke. I am not an ABA therapist, but discrete trial training is a strategy used in ABA programs. In my parent state of mind, I had only one opinion: the teachers in this classroom targeted skills and behaviors and taught in an extremely structured and scripted fashion. When a student accomplished a skill, the teacher rewarded them with whatever was most motivating. Sebastian needed a structured, systematic, sequential learning environment—my graduate studies had taught me that—but having Sebastian sit in a tiny cubby with a teacher who was training him to make eye contact for a potato chip wasn't exactly what I had in mind.

Once we were out of the classroom, John stepped aside, knowing I wouldn't keep silent.

"We don't see the value of Sebastian being in a room with other nonverbal students. And we don't feel he's the type of child who needs this particular kind of intervention. The developmentalist who diagnosed Sebastian didn't even suggest it. His current classroom doesn't use discrete trials, and he's already making progress after just four weeks." I was still trying to figure out why we needed to have this conversation, and then it occurred to me. "Do you have an available spot in the class of twelve?"

"No," she said.

Ah, so we were supposed to buy whatever was on the shelf that day? No thank you. And as if she could read that thought on my face, she said, "We've known your family for a long time, and if you want Sebastian in the class of twelve, we'll do that, but you have to know it's because it's what *you* want and not because it's what the team thinks he needs."

I would never speak to a parent like that. I do not assume to know a child better than their parents. A child's diagnosis should not solely determine their needs. My college professors criticized special education models that relied on remediating deficits and instead taught us to identify a child's strengths and use them to support their weaknesses. This school didn't have any faith in Sebastian's abilities, and I didn't have any faith in theirs.

When we met with the BOE administrator to finalize Sebastian's preschool services, John, typically quiet at these meetings, explained the decision to place our son in the general education preschool. "All our hopes are with this little boy, that he can rise above his disabilities and be able to sit beside his peers in a typical preschool setting. We want to keep the expectations high because Sebastian is our last chance for anything even vaguely resembling normal." I couldn't help but cry for my brave, broken-hearted husband. We had never discussed the fact that we both shared these feelings. Hearing John say these words out loud, to a BOE administrator, renewed a bond I feared had weakened because of his work schedule and the lack of communication that came with it. I'd worried that we were developing a silence that might lead us to the type of quiet, separate-bedroom marriage his parents had shared. But our silence wasn't his parents' silence, and our sons' disabilities hadn't driven us apart.

Nothing proves a person's strength more than their willingness to share vulnerabilities. My mother was the first to teach me this lesson. Widowed with two children at home, she worked day and night. While my mother embraced and modeled a stop-and-smell-the-roses mentality, she cried plenty, cursed my father for leaving her, and yelled at my brother James and me when her frustrations got the best of her. It seemed common in the 1970s to both love and fear your mother. I did, but I never doubted her love for me, and as I got older, I respected her ability to openly display the full range of her emotions.

John's ability to share his honest, vulnerable truth also reminded me of a lesson I learned at Hunter from Jim. He spoke about his most embarrassing moment onstage. "I was up there with a fake Cheshire cat smile plastered on my face. It's the worst thing you can do—mugging. It denies you and the audience an authentic performance." He placed his hand over his heart and with an exhalation softened his chest. "Just stay at home." As a dancer and a parent, it's so much easier to be honest and giving when there are no injuries to contend with. The part of me I'd hoped to ease by having a second child suffered greater injuries now.

It's common for a dancer to perform while injured. When I performed *Missa Brevis* at St. John the Divine, I developed a case of shin splints so severe I couldn't walk. John laughed at me every morning as I shuffled out of bed. I spent the day icing, heating, massaging, stretching, and limping to rehearsal. Onstage, I didn't feel a thing, and not because of ibuprofen or adrenaline. I didn't ignore my injury or overcompensate by stressing other parts of my body. I gave my pain all the attention it deserved, and then put my energies toward accepting all the other parts of my body that were strong and fully capable. Injuries didn't limit my ability to dance because movement comes from who a person is on the inside. When you give an injury more time than it warrants, it devours your appreciation, restricts your freedom, and projects nothing but pain to the audience. Life offstage is very much the same, but I wasn't always smart enough to realize it.

When Sebastian started preschool, he was nonverbal, pointed to the picture board I had made, and used roughly ten formal American Sign Language signs to communicate. His class had a total of fifteen three-year-olds, one teacher, and two assistant teachers. I was secure in the notion that we had found a supportive environment. I enjoyed the simple pleasure of walking Sebastian to school and was ready to experience the positive aspects of having my son included, but I was feeling just a fraction off-center. Exactly the way you feel when you step off a roller coaster ride. If I just kept walking, I was sure I'd regain my equilibrium.

Despite his autism, Sebastian had a well-defined attachment to me, and it took some time to accomplish tearless goodbyes in the morning. He was in school for three days and a total of twenty-one hours a week. The SEIT worked with Sebastian fifteen hours a week. He also received three thirty-minute speech therapy sessions. On his off days, we went to morning music and gym classes and traveled to Manhattan in the afternoons for more speech and occupational therapy at a sensory gym. The ultimate goal was to see him make gains in his individual therapies and to transfer those skills to the classroom setting.

Sebastian received a specialized speech therapy called Prompt, typically used for children who have a speech delay due to oral motor planning problems. Sebastian wasn't considered apraxic, but he did have difficulty forming individual sounds. A Prompt therapist uses a hands-on method to physically prompt the formation of each sound. A touch above the upper lip coupled with verbal models, for example, encouraged the *M* sound. This multisensory technique appealed to me as one who had spent years with dance teachers physically molding me. When a teacher places their hands on your body and sends their energy directly into targeted muscles, all thinking can get out of the way. The only goal is to feel the correction and allow your body to respond. I wanted my son to feel, make new connections, and build stronger pathways.

In the sensory gym, the occupational therapist worked on improving upper extremity strength and sensory processing skills. Sebastian was a sensory seeker. He routinely displayed self-stimulatory behaviors such as jumping, hopping, waving his hand in front of his face, and using random vocalizations. He was giving himself more physical input in an effort to stimulate his senses. I'd compare it to the way the nervous system uses a yawn in an attempt to rouse the brain. Instead of making Sebastian more aware of his surroundings, however, these behaviors caused him to concentrate more intently on himself. He was enthralled with the physical sensations. Imagine chewing a piece of gum to help relieve fatigue when you drive. You wouldn't focus solely on how the gum made you feel and forget the road in front of you. We were striving to help him more appropriately satisfy his need for stimulation while increasing his ability to focus beyond himself.

I incorporated the OT's techniques into our daily home routine. There was a brush to use on Sebastian's extremities, weighted vests for him to wear, and a listening program with special music piped through headphones. Each therapeutic technique had its own protocol, and I followed all of them as closely as I could so I wouldn't feel responsible if any particular technique failed.

My focus was strong, and I continued to follow my instincts. I saw Sebastian's self-stimulatory behaviors as a form of dance. I wondered if Sebastian would be more aware of his actions if I assigned them a more conventional purpose. If he learned about dance, could he use his movement patterns more functionally? I bought ballet DVDs for him to watch and taught him basic steps. At some point all choreographers have to give their dance over to the performers. I hoped to create something that Sebastian could one day make his own.

By January, we were already able to appreciate our efforts. Sebastian was toilet trained and speaking in short phrases. Whenever I caught him absorbed in his self-stimulatory movements, I'd ask him, "What are you doing, Sebastian?"

He would stop, look at me, and say, "I'm dancing."

Sebastian's teachers adored him. His classmates embraced him. It seemed that our gamble on inclusion had paid off. It was satisfying to know that he could make gains in the general education setting. I continued to question all the current techniques used to address autism.

I knew parents who swore by applied behavior analysis. I took no issue with their beliefs. John and I just didn't buy that it was the cure-all. How many countless children used this method without success? It couldn't possibly be the only answer. It was, however, the most widely recognized, scrutinized, and approved form of treatment. Sebastian's progress motivated me to research a relationship-based method called Floortime. In Floortime, you enter the child's world to gain their interest and encourage them to engage with you in a personally meaningful way.

After traveling to Virginia for a four-day Floortime training course, I understood my goal was to help Sebastian *feel* the need to be a part of our family and respond to us because something inside was driving him, not to deliver a scripted response to us because that was what he was trained to do. If he was interested in jumping, then I would jump with him. I connected with actions, like I'd done with my early intervention students. I strove to communicate feelings as I had as a dancer with my audiences. Children tend to take notice when you copy them. Sebastian loved the game of chase and responded well to rough-and-tumble interactions. If he wasn't going to come out and play on his own, we were just going to have to invite ourselves inside. After implementing Floortime strategies into our daily lives as best as we could on our own, I soon discovered we were on the right track.

Sitting in the hallway at Sebastian's school, I spotted him at the end of the long corridor waiting in line for the bathroom. Instead of calling out to him, I decided to wait. I expected the all too familiar moment when he'd walk right by me, oblivious to my existence until I called him. I focused on nothing but my son, standing in line. *Come on, Sebastian, just look at me.* And just like the sappiest scripted fairy-tale moment, his eyes caught mine, and I felt a line connect us. Then a spark as he ran toward me, shouting, "Mommy!"

It wasn't just the fact that he called me. He had already accomplished that. It was the first time he independently responded to my presence physically and verbally without any prompting.

At the end of his first year of preschool, there was no reason to change our strategies. We were concerned, though, because Sebastian's class of fifteen would grow to twenty-five, and twenty-one hours a week would become thirty-five. The BOE increased his SEIT services from fifteen to twenty hours, along with daily speech services and occupational therapy twice a week. Sebastian's November birthday also put him at a clear disadvantage. In addition to his delays, he was younger than most of his classmates. In trendier neighborhoods, parents were holding their children back a year. This type of "redshirting" was vastly unknown in Bay Ridge. I anticipated a difficult transition into kindergarten.

Our ultimate goal was for Sebastian to attend our local zoned school in an inclusion kindergarten classroom. However, this collaborative team-teaching class, taught by a general and special educator, could have more than twenty-five students. Other options included a 6:1:2 (six children, one teacher, two assistants) autistic class, but I worried that those would be filled with nonverbal students. The next option would be a class of twelve. Many parents viewed this class as a disability dumping ground. I did my student teaching in a class of twelve. I will never forget watching a veteran teacher struggle to meet the needs of a screaming five-year-old, a learning disabled seven-year-old, a cognitively and physically disabled six-year-old, and a child who banged her head on the wall out of frustration.

The BOE did have a new specialized inclusion program that grouped four "high-functioning" autistic children with eight typically developing students. Thinking this was a perfect solution, I spoke to a program supervisor. She asked, "Do you know the criteria for the program?"

"No, please tell me."

"Your son has to be on the spectrum."

"Okay."

"He has to be on grade level."

"Yup."

"He can't have any behavioral or attention difficulties."

No behavioral or attention difficulties? Have you met a child on the spectrum? I wasn't sure if I was more offended as a parent or an educator, but I got the message. This was a new program, and in order to make it succeed, they would need to accept only "perfect" children with disabilities.

Sebastian was not a perfect child. He was hyperactive and known from time to time to run away if another child cried. I often referred to him as my flight risk. I think this constituted a behavior problem. He also had significant attention difficulties. He was learning the basic preschool skills but needed constant prompting to complete tasks. The only thing he could independently stay focused on was his love and obsession for Cinderella.

After some hesitation on our part, Sebastian had come to acquire a collection of princess dolls that was the envy of all his female cousins, while also somewhat horrifying the more traditional members of John's family. All we knew was Sebastian would do almost anything in order to play with Cinderella. While

I could deal with Sebastian carrying his dolls around in public and the sight of Cinderella cake toppers littering every drawer in our home, I wasn't liberal-minded enough to buy him a frilly princess dress. He'd gravitate to them in the stores, stroke the tulle, and say, "Please." I had to draw the line. He could look, but that was all. I'd witnessed enough shoppers side-eyeing Sebastian.

More than once, John argued with me, "Just buy it for him." His more liberal attitude didn't surprise me. When we applied for our marriage license, he said, "You don't have to change your name. I don't own you." I wasn't proud of my no-dress stance. Coming from the world of modern dance, I knew men who wore dresses better than I did. I'm a jeans and T-shirt kind of gal. I just couldn't bear the thought of Sebastian frolicking around in a princess dress and strangers judging him more than they already were.

With Cinderella as a constant companion, Sebastian made a smooth start to his second year of preschool. His inclusionary success led me to make a career shift. In addition to my early intervention cases, I began working as an itinerant teacher in local preschools. I was thrilled to play a part in a family's desire to keep their child included in the general education setting.

Just as we were both settling into our new environments, Sebastian's teacher quit. It was difficult for him, and I sensed there were problems between the new teacher and Sebastian's SEIT. One of the most difficult aspects of teaching is learning to work with multiple adults in your classroom. It's not always easy for an itinerant teacher to implement special education strategies to a single student in a general education classroom without stepping on the other teacher's toes. No one would tell me what the conflict was, but Sebastian grew less interested in listening to the SEIT.

The communication notebook that the SEIT used to write Sebastian's daily progress focused on his growing behavioral problems. The SEIT wanted me to implement consequences at home if Sebastian didn't comply with her at school. I didn't feel it was reasonable to punish him at home for something that had happened hours earlier. The school's director and I agreed that Sebastian's behaviors needed immediate attention at school. I was prepared to reinforce teacher expectations but not with a system of negative discipline.

I agreed to create a reward system at home for good school behavior. If Sebastian had a good day, the SEIT would draw a happy face in the notebook, and I would allow him to watch a movie before bed. It was a simple plan, but nothing is that simple. Every time I looked in the book, I dreaded the sight of a sad face next to the proclamation of all Sebastian's naughty deeds. As the negative reports increased, my anxieties grew into frustration. I tried to discuss each day's problems with Sebastian. He had enough language to answer questions about his behavior appropriately. Is it okay to hit the teacher? No. He clearly understood right from wrong. He just didn't have enough skills to resolve his behavioral inconsistencies. I was powerless to rectify the battles at school. Our home became a new front line. If Sebastian couldn't watch a movie at night, he thought I was punishing him. He would tantrum, and I would yell at him about the SEIT's notes.

Benjamin was my heartbreak. Sebastian tested my sanity.

What kind of parent are you, scolding an autistic four-year-old for behaviors he can't control?

I can't control my pain. My mother didn't control her frustration. I know Sebastian feels my love for him, just like I always felt my mother's love for me.

You don't have to do things the way your mother did them. She had good reason to yell at you. She was a single parent.

I'm as good as a single parent with the amount of time and physical support I get from John.

But you have a master's degree in special education. You know how to deal with behavior problems. Use what you've learned.

Stay at Home

I can't always be perfect. I have too much on my plate.
You're full of excuses. You disgust me. Stop whining and figure out
how to break the cycle.

I didn't have time to break the cycle. In addition to the pressures of Sebastian's behaviors and figuring out his transition to kindergarten, I was bracing for Benjamin's next surgery. Unlike his two previous tendon lengthening surgeries, this scoliosis surgery would be long and risky. His orthopedic surgeon planned to slice open Benjamin's back, place two bars along his entire spine, and fuse each vertebra. Fifteen days before Benjamin's eighth birthday, I placed him on an operating table. The room was cold and crowded with people and equipment. Although I was dressed in a hospital jumpsuit, shoe covers, hat, and mask, I was afraid to touch anything in the sterile environment. I wanted to cradle my son, but I had given him away. As much as he was mine, this team of strangers owned him now.

I leaned in close to Benjamin. He stared into my eyes. I didn't spew an earful of lies about everything being all right. I told him the only truths I knew at that moment, "You're the best boy. Be brave. Mommy and Daddy will be waiting for you. We love you BenjaboyD." I fought to steady my voice while singing one of his favorite songs, "Take Me Out to the Ball Game." He cried when the anesthesiologist placed the mask over his face. I kissed him repeatedly until he slipped into unconsciousness.

A nurse said, "Okay, Mommy, you can go. We'll call you when he's out of surgery." I didn't want to leave Benjamin. My feet began to move, but my mind ran one last lap of insecurity. I imagined the surgical team sticking him with needles, placing him on his stomach, and coaxing his rigid arms outward in a crucifix position. His recovery would be painful. He wasn't prepared for this. I imagined how confused, betrayed, and miserable he would feel when he woke. It was all just so unfair to him. We'd done everything from therapy to bracing to avoid this surgery, but

Benjamin's muscles bent his spine to a 62-degree curve. I left the room worried about prolonged anesthesia and the likelihood of blood transfusions, post-op infections, and seizures. I wondered if we'd celebrate Benjamin's eighth birthday or plan a funeral.

John and I paced the hospital floors clinging to our cell phones. Six hours later, we went out for some fresh air. As we walked the streets of Manhattan, I looked up to heaven. *Please, God, watch over Benjamin. Give the doctors the strength to get him through this. Don't take him from me.*

John interrupted my silent prayer. "Should we try to have some lunch?"

"I guess. Not that I'm hungry. When are they going to call?"

"No news is good news."

"No news means we just haven't gotten the bad news yet."

"Hey, I'm the negative one. Don't let me rub off on you."

"You're not."

"Thanks for going into the OR. I would have if you didn't want to, but I really didn't want to."

"It's okay. I don't know if I could have stayed behind. I know we're doing the right thing, but I really wish we could have spared him this surgery."

"Nature isn't going to spare Benjamin."

"Nope, and nothing is stronger than nature. I can't imagine how I could live if something happened and we lost Benjamin. But sometimes I think about all the children who died when I was in the Internet group. In a way, I envy those families. They get to move on while we just keep moving."

"Sometimes I wonder why Benjamin is still here."

"Sometimes I think he's here because without him, I'd go insane. Seriously, all I have to do is hear Benjamin's laughter and he takes me right out of a Sebastian-induced funk."

The fact that John and I could confess these thoughts to each other without apologies or explanations comforted me. Ten and a half hours after I left Benjamin on the operating table, a nurse called us, and we raced to see our son. I felt as though I'd just jumped from a plane. Plummeting to the earth, filled with excitement and terror as I reach for the parachute cord, wondering if it would open.

The surgeon met us with X-rays of Benjamin's new spine. I stared at all the strange hardware and screws jutting this way and that. *This man isn't a doctor; he's a master carpenter.* Other than two units of blood and one moment of unstable blood pressure, all had gone well. As we headed to the recovery room, I remembered the doctor's earlier warning: "His face will be very swollen from lying on his stomach for so long."

To our surprise, Benjamin wasn't bloated at all. John and I surrounded his bed. I whispered, "Hey, beauty boy." Benjamin managed through his pained and medicated daze to shock us with a brief but most definite smile. It was the greatest example of vulnerability and strength I had ever witnessed.

For seven days, I took the day shifts in the ICU while John was at work. He'd come straight from the office and sit vigil every night. My mother maintained a steady presence at home with Sebastian. We had balance. Then John went back to his production coordinator life. After a four-week hiatus tending to Benjamin at home, I went back to teaching and worrying about Sebastian's educational future.

There was no doubt in my mind that Sebastian's behavior would be the deciding factor in his upcoming kindergarten placement. I needed to get a handle on the situation quickly. I looked to the general education staff at the preschool. They adored Sebastian and had nothing but good things to say. I was conflicted. How could he be fine in the eyes of the general educators and a disaster in the eyes of the SEIT? My emotions bounced between anxiety and anger on a daily basis. Was the SEIT's behavior influencing Sebastian's performance? To be fair,

I knew how infuriating he could be, but as a teacher, if you let your emotions guide your actions, you will be ineffective. Was she overwhelmed, frustrated, completely disappointed because he wasn't progressing as much as he had the previous year, or was she simply burned out?

I had no idea exactly how the SEIT was conducting herself in the classroom, but I was tired of the hushed hallway conversations with the staff about nonspecific conflicts between the head general education teacher and the SEIT. I couldn't decide if I was being overly sensitive and judgmental or if I had a legitimate gripe. Was I just angry because things weren't going as I had hoped? Was I assigning blame because I wanted to avoid feeling responsible for Sebastian's evolving failure? Should we have placed him in a special education classroom? Would the expectations have been too low there?

We couldn't go back in time. Sebastian was making his own progress. Wasn't it important to give him academic opportunities with nondisabled peers? I hated that my original uncertainties had resurfaced. They leached into every moment I spent with my son. I was harboring a nasty sense that, as much as I loved Sebastian, I didn't always like him. No guilt could run deeper for a mother. I couldn't stand the toxic loop that my emotions were running. Was it too much to ask to get through an entire week without one of us having a major meltdown?

In an effort to reduce Sebastian's stress, I decided to pick him up earlier. On the first day of this experiment, I arrived unannounced. I thought I'd get a moment to observe before surprising him, but another student ratted me out. "Sebastian, your mommy's here."

Behind a partition I heard the voice of the SEIT, "Good, now your mom will see how you behave." I bit my lip as she gave me the details of that day's offense. I mentally dodged her anger like a germ I didn't care to catch. I was finished judging Sebastian by her standards. I brought him home without referencing the event, and the rest of the evening was calm. I grew somber at the thought of how difficult his little life was. I fought not to think about the long-term implications of the pain I had caused him. My mind was wandering in a hallway of defeat. I searched for a welcome mat.

I discussed some of Sebastian's noncompliant behaviors with his occupational therapist at the sensory gym. Aubrey was a brilliant young OT who had a remarkable grasp of Sebastian's development. She never seemed frustrated by his occasional hitting or general lack of following directions. She invested in his achievements and never demonstrated a hint of negativity. Among our many thoughtful conversations, she taught me a lesson I still use personally and professionally. Children with disabilities make developmental gains on their own timeline. Often, they make a leap in one area while other areas lag behind. It's difficult to have such unbalanced skills.

We both acknowledged that we frequently saw developmental growth spurts followed by regression. Then she asked me to imagine how unsettling a growth spurt would feel. I thought about how I would cope with making rapid and dramatic internal changes. Every time Sebastian gained a new set of skills, he had to acclimate to all those new abilities and deal with generalizing them across environments. With all the changes he'd made in the last two years of therapy he must have felt constantly overwhelmed. I could relate.

I thought about something I learned at the Floortime training. "In order to expect a child to work at the top of their box, you have to work at the top of yours." Parents and teachers have to act in an optimal way in order to influence and bring out the best behaviors in a child. I couldn't expect Sebastian to make the right behavioral choices while his teacher antagonized him.

When contemplating kindergarten options, I had Sebastian reevaluated. The psychologist disagreed with the autism diagnosis. He felt Sebastian had a severe language disability coupled with a sensory integration disorder. John was skeptical about this new diagnosis. Autism better explained his underdeveloped relationship with Sebastian. I bought right into the psychologist's point of view. I put a blanket over the autism diagnosis and allowed myself to drift back into my original state of denial.

I was a professional rationalizer, but all my defense mechanisms couldn't shield my heart from feeling the truth. Only once did I discuss Sebastian's disabilities with another parent at school. I wanted him to fit in, but he needed so much support in order to socialize with other children. Having Sebastian included in the "normal" classroom didn't make him normal.

Sebastian had gained his own form of acceptance in the school community. He looked like every other kid to the untrained eye, at least for some amount of time. I was the one who couldn't acclimate. It was similar to my earlier experiences with Benjamin in the playground. We had every right to be there, but I didn't feel like we belonged. It was a self-imposed mental outcasting. I always felt as if I were perpetuating a fallacy by avoiding the conversation with the other parents. Sebastian's autism was the dirty little secret I was keeping—from them and from myself.

I needed to see Sebastian for who he was, an evolving, beautiful, four-year-old boy who, despite his gains, still had major challenges to overcome. He needed guidance and, as trying as he could be, I would have to forgive him for testing me every single day. On the days I couldn't be patient enough, when I was an ordinary struggling parent who was still getting it wrong, I would have to absolve myself.

If Sebastian were one of my students, he would be fascinating to work with. There was never a day when I didn't witness his progress. Even though I didn't know how it would serve him, his strengths were clear in relation to dance. Mesmerized by his growing collection of ballet DVDs, including *Swan Lake, Romeo and Juliet, Giselle, Coppélia, Cinderella, Don Quixote, La Sylphide, Raymonda,* and *The Firebird,* he danced in front of the television, copying the choreographic moves. He enjoyed books about the ballet storylines and would stage his own productions with paper dolls as he hummed entire musical scores.

Sebastian was always in motion. Often as he pranced around the house, John would tell him, "Sebastian, please relax."

He would stop only long enough to scold back, "Don't say that, Daddy. I love to dance."

None of this eased my mind about the kindergarten options. John and I still agreed an inclusionary class was the only placement to strive for.

When Sebastian's Turning Five Team made their classroom observations, he answered all their questions, and his SEIT joked that, next to his peers, "Sebastian couldn't be picked out of a lineup." A few weeks later, I met with a district administrator to discuss kindergarten program options. I thought about Sebastian's latest psychological evaluation. I knew the speech delay diagnosis was wishful thinking, but I honestly didn't think an autism program would fit his needs. Without John at the meeting, I straightened my back and held my torso stiff like a knight prepared for battle. I did not share Sebastian's earlier autism diagnosis. It was an unspoken rule in New York that a child with an autism classification would not be educated in the inclusionary collaborative team teaching program. The administrator classified Sebastian as speech impaired and offered the CTT class with speech and occupational therapies.

I should have been celebrating, but deep down, I knew nothing positive would ever come from an inauthentic performance. Insincerity is far worse than screwing up choreography. You might be able to fool an audience, but you can't lie to yourself forever. The greatest sins are those you commit with full awareness.

10

Stillness Isn't Static

A time to cast away stones,
and a time to gather stones together

In August 2007, seven months after Benjamin's scoliosis surgery, John placed him in his feeding chair and forgot to fasten
the lap belt. He walked two feet away to get Benjamin's drink
and heard a crash. Somehow Benjamin, a child with minimal
ability to move, had fallen forward and hit the wooden floor.
Unable to put his hands out to protect himself, he'd landed on
his face and knees.

I was in Manhattan when John called. "I'm on the way to the
emergency room. Ben needs his lip stitched." I raced to my car,
pounded the steering wheel, and unleashed a beautifully mastered
collection of profanities. This whole situation never would have
happened if we'd stuck to the original plan. I had the babysitter
all lined up to take care of Benjamin so I could get fingerprinted
for work, but at the last minute, John's work schedule changed,
and I canceled the sitter. He should have taken my suggestion to
leave Benjamin home with the sitter and come hang out with me
for a fun day in the city. *Joanne, don't be angry with John. If it had*
happened on your watch, you wouldn't want him to hold it against
you. He's going to hate himself enough for the both of you.

Several stitches and facial X-rays later, we hoped the worst part of the fall was behind us. It wasn't. As the days went by, Benjamin grew more and more uncomfortable during diaper changes. Whenever we lifted him or placed him in bed at night, he screamed. Based on his every minor negative response to handling, we adjusted our lifting technique and placed extra pillows under his head, legs, and arms. No amount of support eased him. I was certain some of his spinal hardware had shifted, but a series of X-rays proved me wrong. None of his doctors could find the source of Benjamin's pain.

Benjamin's inability to speak frustrates and frightens me most when he's hurting. Something as routine as appendicitis could kill him if I'm not smart enough to figure it out. We treated him with anti-inflammatory medications and hoped that one day the crying would stop. One, two, three weeks went by. None of the methods we used to distract him during seizures helped: singing, dancing, the sound of running water, books, Telletubbies, Clifford, kisses.

John would clench his teeth and shriek, "Fuck me! Fuck my life! This is how I know there's no God!"

I didn't want to hear about his lack of faith or witness his unrelenting self-blame. I was dealing with my own hell. Every time Benjamin cried, Sebastian ran screaming. Like dealing with a colicky baby, I decided it was better to just close Benjamin's door and walk away until he calmed himself. I would return begging, "Please forgive me, Benjamin. I don't know what else to do." What kind of mother turns away from her child when he's in pain? I was beginning to understand why a mother would load her children into a car and drive into a lake.

I wanted to be Benjamin's hero. I rummaged through every bit of knowledge I had retained from years of studying anatomy, kinesiology, and biology. I summonsed long-lost memories from every dance teacher, physical therapist, chiropractor, and massage therapist I had ever encountered. How could Benjamin be in this much pain with no diagnosis or resolution in sight? Hadn't I watched enough medical mystery shows on television to figure this out? What was I missing? How long would we all be punished? One unfastened strap had changed our lives from manageable to unbearable. How many lessons could we learn in a lifetime? How often would life throw Benjamin's fragility in our faces? I marked the calendar each day to document Benjamin's level of pain.

In September, Benjamin tolerated diaper changes and grimaced less when we lifted him. I welcomed this resolution because the start of a new school year is stressful enough, and we'd scheduled Benjamin for a minor soft tissue foot surgery in October. Also on my list of things to be grateful for was Sebastian's smooth transition into his inclusion kindergarten class. I enjoyed watching Sebastian line up with the neighborhood kids every morning. He fit right in with his light blue polo shirt and uniform shorts. Like a stage mother sending her child off to audition, I gave him last minute instructions, then waved and blew kisses as he disappeared into the building behind the two teachers paired for the mix of general and special education students.

One month into the school year, when Benjamin was recovering from surgery, Sebastian's teachers requested John and I come in for a meeting.

The kindergarten classroom was overcrowded with desks, chairs, and learning centers. The teachers invited us to sit by Sebastian's desk. I was surprised they'd placed him so close to the door. When I met them in June, at the kindergarten orientation, I warned them about his undocumented autism spectrum disorder and history of running out of the classroom.

Ms. Alter, the general educator, took the lead: "Sebastian's having some trouble following directions and the daily routine."

John looked to me to respond for both of us. I scanned the

environment. Posters and classwork occupied every inch of wall space. Even I felt incapable of taking it all in. "That's not surprising, considering his language delays. He's always needed directions repeated, and time to process."

She continued, "How hard do you want us to push Sebastian?"

This question seemed odd coming from such seasoned teachers. I gave John a quick, concerned look. The educator in me spoke up. "We want Sebastian to be an active, learning member of the classroom community. You'll need to use your best judgment to keep him engaged without frustrating him. Reward systems might work, or perhaps you can pair him up with other students."

She said, "We have a meeting every day, and the children share their morning news. Can you give Sebastian something to talk about? It's difficult for him to come up with anything."

Ms. Banks, the special educator, nodded.

I said, "Sure, I can do that. I'll even write it out for him, using pictures to help him read."

As John and I left the building, he said, "This is going to be a problem. What do you think?"

I said, "I hope not. When I met them last June, they told me they'd taught many children on the spectrum and that they'd seen it all and knew what they were doing. Now they seem lost. I feel like they ignored my suggestions. Why not give him a buddy to work with? It's a basic inclusion classroom strategy."

Sebastian and I pieced stories together every evening, but a sick feeling in the pit of my stomach was hard to ignore. *What if this doesn't help? You put him in this class hoping for the best, but have you set him up to fail? Just because you want him to belong doesn't mean he does.* Every morning I stood outside the school building, feeling as though my dreams were slipping away and I was letting Sebastian down.

The following week, Sebastian ran out of the classroom. The teachers wanted me to implement consequences at home if it happened again. I still didn't believe it was appropriate to punish Sebastian for school behaviors, but running from the classroom was a serious problem, so I threatened to hold his Cinderella doll hostage if he bolted from his teachers again.

The educator in me wanted to know the cause of Sebastian's behaviors. Was he running to avoid work? Was he afraid of something? Did he want to go somewhere specific? If they could determine the cause, they could devise a plan of action. I knew Sebastian was not their only challenge, and they were overwhelmed. I just didn't want to be in a position where I was punishing my son because of his disabilities and the school's inability to meet his needs.

Sebastian's beloved blonde princess couldn't keep him from his fleeing ways. Two days after his first running episode, he did it again. Four days after that, I received a phone call from Ms. Alter.

"Sebastian is fine, but we briefly lost him. He escaped from the lunchroom when the monitor took her eyes off him." I was unable to formulate a G-rated response, so I kept silent. Ms. Alter continued, "We searched for him both inside and outside the school. Fortunately, a teacher on the fifth floor noticed him running in the hallway." Unlike my Brooklyn Catholic high school, there were no locks or guards on Sebastian's school doors. I pictured him running toward the nearby highway and his broken body flung by a speeding vehicle. I shook the image from my mind but then envisioned Sebastian lost in a world incapable of understanding him.

The following day, Ms. Banks informed me that the school was assigning a temporary one-to-one paraprofessional to work with Sebastian. Last spring when I sat with the district administrator for Sebastian's Turning Five IEP meeting, I mentioned the need for a one-to-one, but the administrator said, "We expect a child referred to a collaborative team teaching class to manage without that type of support." In fear of losing the CTT placement, I gave up the debate, hoping for the best and knowing I could request additional services later if needed.

Sebastian's favorite game was chase, and he was not ready to give up on the fun, although I learned there was one legitimate, predictable cause of this behavior. Another student, Veronica, had developed the unfortunate habit of daily tantrums. At the end of October, the teachers requested another meeting.

John refused to come. "I'm swamped after taking off for the last meeting and Ben's surgery. You don't need me." When there's a conflict at school, I believe it's best to show a united parental front, but maybe not at the risk of stressing out an already sleep-deprived, overworked, edgy husband. Still, it annoyed me that John had the option to not balance work and Sebastian's educational needs on any given day. My job gave me the freedom to create and manipulate my schedule as I needed, but I had to make up every minute I missed for Benjamin's illnesses and Sebastian's meetings.

I brought Sebastian to an early morning conference with his teachers. Upon our arrival, the secretary escorted us to the principal's office. With zero fond memories of my grammar school principal's office and knowing principals don't typically attend team meetings, I braced for a confrontation. The principal, assistant principal, and Sebastian's teachers filed in and sat with us at a large rectangular table.

"Sebastian's running episodes are a real safety issue," the principal began.

I said, "I agree."

She proceeded, "How do you feel the CTT setting is working?"

It was clear. Sebastian was on trial. I nudged the parent within me aside and summoned the special education advocate. I pulled out my legal pad, gave Sebastian a few blank sheets and a pencil, and asked him to draw some pictures. I needed him occupied so I could focus on the judge and jury. I also wanted to distract him. Even if Sebastian didn't grasp what all the grown-ups sitting around him were saying, I didn't want him to feel unwanted.

I addressed the principal sitting at the far end of the table. "I know Sebastian has problems with his time-on-task and social skills." I quickly turned the question to the teachers sitting across from me. "How do you feel about his current placement?"

Ms. Alter began, "He does need one-to-one assistance in order to attend, but he is learning. He's getting the information."

I took notes: *General educator doesn't seem concerned about academic abilities.*

The principal spoke again. "We don't feel the setting is working for him. He needs a small class size. This school does not have that type of program to offer."

Right then, I knew she was not fluent in special education law. Even if this were a formal IEP meeting, discussing placement at the top of the agenda proved she had predetermined Sebastian's needs.

I leaned forward. "I don't believe the public school's smaller class is appropriate."

She proceeded, "You can look at three settings."

I repeated, "I don't feel it is appropriate. My husband and I want Sebastian in the least restrictive environment given his known strengths."

Inclusion has been an ongoing battle in special education. Children with disabilities didn't have a legal right to a public school education until 1975, but segregation became the norm. Parents fought back and demanded placement in general education classes. The children were not expected to function at grade level. Times have changed, and I fear the gap between general and special education students has grown wider. States are setting inappropriate educational goals. Sebastian's school required an incoming kindergartener to write his full name in upper and lowercase letters. I'm sure some kids could do it, but it's not a developmentally appropriate expectation.

The principal stayed on track. "You have options and can get a parent advocate and ask for a private school setting."

This is where John might have been useful. Even though he's generally quiet at meetings, there's a different tone when he sits at the table. The principal might have been a little less inclined to ignore my remarks. I took a deep breath and looked right into her eyes. "There's a long distance between his current placement and an alternative setting. Why aren't we discussing his need for a one-to-one para?"

Sebastian's teachers exhaled in relief, and one of them asked me to write a formal request to reopen the case. As I steadied my shaking hand to scribble out the letter, the principal commented, "I don't understand why he wasn't given a one-to-one from the beginning. How did he even end up here?"

She was a new principal, but it was more than discouraging that she had so little knowledge about her special education students.

"The district sent a social worker to observe Sebastian. The current mandates were recommended by the Committee on Special Education," I briefed her.

She said, "They saw him here?"

"No. They saw him at his preschool last spring," I explained.

I turned to Sebastian's teachers. "Let's talk about the problem Sebastian's having with the other student's daily meltdowns."

"I only became aware of this issue two weeks ago," the principal said. "I observed this student having a tantrum, and Sebastian was literally shaking. My heart was broken. I couldn't sleep that night." I gave her credit for keeping Veronica's name confidential, but she wasn't getting any sympathy from me. Her loss of sleep was due to her ineffective leadership skills.

I turned my attention away from her and asked the teachers, "How is Sebastian's school counselor working during his therapy sessions to alleviate his anxiety? I don't think he understands how to ask for help, and he can't calm himself down. At this point, the other student doesn't even have to tantrum. Sebastian anticipates her outbursts. He doesn't want to come to school. He tells me she's scary."

Ms. Banks said, "The situation is difficult. We're working on it."

Ms. Alter added, "We've noticed that Sebastian has a habit of smelling books, waving his hands in front of his face, and pacing around."

These aren't atypical behaviors for children on the autistic spectrum. I expected they would know this. I said, "Yes, he's a sensory seeker. Have you discussed this with his occupational therapist? I'm happy to put you in touch with his other OT at the sensory gym. Perhaps she can suggest some strategies to implement in the classroom to help Sebastian work more independently."

The morning bell was about to ring. I kissed Sebastian goodbye and watched him walk to class with his teachers. He was so small between them. That afternoon they approached me. Ms. Alter spoke for them both. "We had no idea the principal was going to suggest a change in placement. We thought she was only going to address the running episodes. We were so surprised." I believed them and was glad they'd have extra help in the classroom.

As a parent, I wanted the CTT placement to work, but my Brooklyn streetwise shit-sensor had me looking over my shoulder. I would collaborate with the teachers, but I was not going to let my optimism blind all my doubts. From the very start, I kept a running record of every interaction with the school, gathering proof of their inability to provide Sebastian with his legal right to a free and appropriate public education. But this had to work. There was no Plan B.

The last time I was this unwilling to devise a backup plan was in the days leading up to my audition for Limón. One of my teachers asked me, "Joanne, what are you going to do if she doesn't pick you?" She, the Limón director, had watched me for two years studying with a dozen Limón teachers. In exchange for classes, I washed mirrors, took attendance, and mended costumes backstage during a summer intensive. She invited me to perform on tour as part of the *Missa Brevis* ensemble. She was going to determine my acceptance into the Limón Company, but everyone knew she had eyes on another dancer. Melora had traveled the globe with a list of impressive dance companies, but I chose to believe there was still hope. I thought Limón was my destiny. I didn't want to admit hard work doesn't always lead to desired outcomes. Not then, and not now.

In early December, the teachers requested another meeting. I begged John to come with me, but he was dealing with a crisis at work. He promised to join in by phone, but it was little consolation. I knew John couldn't bear the weight of one more stressor, but my strength and stamina were breaking down from my daily schedule:

4:30 a.m.: John wakes, showers, and leaves for work.

4–5:00 a.m.: Sebastian wakes. Try to convince him to let me sleep.

6:00 a.m.: Feed Sebastian. Pack Benjamin's breakfast and both their lunches.

6:30 a.m.: Wake Benjamin. Undress, diaper, dress, and carefully affix foot orthotics. Wait for morning seizure to subside so he can swallow three anticonvulsants. Carry him down a flight of stairs and place him in his wheelchair. Strap the lap belt and abductor wedge to keep his knees apart. Fight his stiff arms to get his coat on. Secure the chest harness and four-foot straps. Pray that his transportation nurse finds parking before the school bus arrives at 7:00 a.m.

7:00 a.m.: Shower, dress, and eat. Pack for work.

8:15 a.m.: Listen to Sebastian complaining about going to school as we walk the four blocks.

8:40 a.m.: Walk to work.

2:00 p.m.: Finish work.

3:00 p.m.: Pick up Sebastian, listen to teachers give reports of noncompliance.

3:30 p.m.: Take Benjamin off his bus. Get him out of the wheelchair and set him up in front of the TV in his stander for one hour. Call my friend Debbie to share parenting war stories and vent about husbands.

4:30 p.m.: Start homework with Sebastian. Argue over the fact that he doesn't know what he's doing because he doesn't pay attention to his teachers. Make dinner, feed Benjamin, clean up. Carry Benjamin upstairs, bathe, dress, and read to him. Read to Sebastian.

8:30 p.m.: Lights out for both boys. Exercise. Write session notes, reports, respond to parent emails.

11:30 p.m.: Pass out before John gets home at God knows what hour.

On the day of the meeting, I dialed John's number and placed my open flip phone in the center of the empty table. It wasn't a great connection, which only made the distance between us even wider.

Ms. Alter began, "The addition of the para has had a negative effect on Sebastian. The more she tries to keep him focused, the more frustrated he gets. We're not concerned with his actual academic knowledge. When he does participate, he displays a solid base."

I scribbled notes. It was the best way to avoid making eye contact and divert my welling emotions. Ms. Banks said, "Sebastian is safe with us. We love him, but he's not happy. If you were to observe him, you would be sad for him." I gripped my pen and held my breath. The words on the page blurred.

John broke the silence. "Where does Sebastian go from here?" His voice was tight and professional, a sign that his faith in a positive outcome was broken.

Ms. Banks said, "The school psychologist will complete her testing, and as a team, we'll make a program recommendation. We agree with you; the public school's smaller classes aren't appropriate. Sebastian needs a gentler environment without students who have behavioral problems."

I spoke up, "The only public school alternative is the autism program. I'm concerned Sebastian won't have the right peer models there, and he doesn't need an ABA program."

Ms. Banks nodded her head. "You should start looking around at private schools. Take your time. The district will give you three public school placement options. You must tour them and turn them down. We had a student last year who moved to The HeartShare School in Bensonhurst. His mother fought for it. The district can be convinced to pay for a private school placement."

Three months into the CTT experiment, and it was a complete failure. I couldn't believe both my children would need to be educated outside of our home district and that public school wasn't even a good fit for Sebastian. As an educator, I accepted that NYC was too big to accommodate everyone and every disability, especially the indefinite variations of students with autism. I questioned my ideals about inclusion and my role as an SEIT. I wasn't sure if I should continue working within a model that sometimes failed so miserably.

Ms. Alter added, "Sebastian needs to be in a classroom where they can play Cinderella music all day." It stung, the way all unnecessarily painful things do. As frustrating as Sebastian was, she had no right to tell us he belonged in a world of make-believe. He was capable of more. Should John and I be happy with the picture of Sebastian prancing around a classroom for the rest of his life, uninterested and unable to learn? No. In a classic case of not wanting my child to make the same mistakes I did, I would never encourage Sebastian to limit himself, even when everyone else has given up on him. One of the few regrets I owned was limiting myself to Limón.

I went home and transcribed the meeting notes onto the running record. My son's failure was my own. I treated it like any other disappointing performance. I stood in front of the mirror retracing my steps. Every time I caught myself making the same mistake, I'd growl. *What is wrong with you? Why can't you fix what you're doing?* Perseverating on the negative doesn't teach you how to solve the problem. It reinforces defeat. The goal should be to retrain your way of thinking and acting, but I was strengthening improper pathways.

My teacher and parent halves revisited an old debate.

You knew inclusion was risky, but you put him in there anyway.

He didn't belong in the other programs.

Like ABA? Are you sure he wouldn't have succeeded there?

He's always made progress without it.

But it's still the most widely accepted form of remediation.

I didn't see the need to limit him to a strategy that doesn't help every single child on the endless spectrum of autism.

But he's failing.

So I'm to blame because I've made all the decisions?
Well, John didn't.
He agreed.
What choice did he have? He only sees Sebastian on the weekends. They barely have a relationship.
Is that my fault too? John understands his son's needs.
Good luck finding an autism-friendly school that isn't ABA. Sebastian's life and happiness is on you.
Ms. Banks's description of Sebastian weighed me down. "He runs away from work and stares out the window. He's not interacting with anyone." I scrolled through the pages of the running record, proof I had created a sad, lonely boy. Even if I deleted the file, I couldn't erase my mistakes.

In January, the school psychologist called to schedule an EPC. "Can we meet next week?"

"What's an EPC?" I asked.

"It's an education planning conference. You requested it. Our findings suggest Sebastian needs more support than we can give. The meeting is to make placement recommendations. I sat with Sebastian, and he knew his numbers and letters, but he wouldn't relate to me. That's enough to make a recommendation."

It wasn't enough. I'm sure she planned to rely on Sebastian's autism diagnosis, but our doctors had never documented his autism, and school teams cannot make a diagnosis. So if this was her polite way of telling me she was ready to give him that label and kick him to the curb, she was lacking. Sebastian is usually responsive to adults. His teachers reported that he loved leaving the classroom with his therapists. I'd only been talking to Ms. Lacking Compassion for a few minutes, and I could understand why Sebastian had deemed her unworthy of his attention. I couldn't relate to her either.

"I was told you took Sebastian to NYU for a psychiatric evaluation. Correct? Can I have that report?"

She was after that diagnosis. The defensive advocate side of my brain fired up. John and I had every intention of sharing the report, even though we were under no obligation to do so. "I am currently pursuing the written report. I think it is essential to have everything completed in order to make an informed decision about Sebastian's placement needs. We will not schedule a meeting until we have time to review the evaluations. My husband and I both work, and we can't be available on such short notice anyway."

She said, "Fine. I'll wait for the report."

She had no choice. It's one thing to have a general-education-minded principal who disregards special education law, but for a school psychologist to ignore our rights was unforgivable.

- We had the right to an independent evaluation such as the psychiatric.
- Sebastian had a right to a fair and objective comprehensive evaluation from the school.
- We had a right to see their reports before an IEP meeting.
- A written invitation to the IEP meeting was required.
- They are required to give us reasonable time and accommodations for the meeting.
- The invitation should have come with a copy of our legal rights.
- They never added the para to the IEP.
- They never offered a behavior plan to address his running and general lack of compliance.
- The teachers should not have recommended The HeartShare School. Only the placement office can make recommendations.

I don't like it when people disregard the rules, but I noted all of it in the running record. These were the types of procedural mistakes that would help us win a private school placement. I decided it was time to hire a lawyer and found a woman who had previously been a special educator. John and I reviewed Sebastian's case with her. She advised us to continue documenting school interactions and researching private school options.

While we waited for the report and school recommendations from NYU, I grilled my friends, colleagues, and a former Hunter College professor who'd just retired as a BOE administrator about public and private schools. I did everything possible in order to put Sebastian on the right track, but the options were intangible. I hoped the lawyer would relieve my sense of doom. Having her on board was empowering but restrictive. I had to report every step, and every action required preapproval. Sebastian's school team didn't know we had retained a lawyer. I was collecting mistakes to throw back at them later. Every conversation with his teachers reminded me of my inauthentic performance at Sebastian's Turning Five meeting.

Two months had passed since Sebastian's NYU evaluation, and I still couldn't get the written report, so I took Sebastian to a neuropsychologist for a more comprehensive educational evaluation.

At the end of January, we received an invitation in the mail to a "Promotion in Doubt" meeting. I noted its arrival in the running record. I noted the second notice the teachers sent home in Sebastian's bag. And the third, left in my mail slot in a handwritten, unsealed, unstamped envelope. I ripped that one up. My son wasn't the failure. The system was failing him. I showed up at school for the obligatory meeting.

Ms. Banks said, "Sorry about the letters. We didn't send them. They're automatically generated."

I got it. Teachers are notoriously powerless within the system and do all the dirty work. Parents have the stronger voice, which is why it's important to work together.

"Sebastian is resistant to come to the rug for stories. He won't complete phonics lessons unless I sit with him. He wanders the classroom and plays alone."

Ms. Alter interrupted, "Except we have seen him play chase with Veronica."

Ms. Banks added, "We can't believe he likes to do that. He's still so frightened when she tantrums. Although he doesn't like it when we try to stop her. He even covers my mouth when I try to speak to her."

Ms. Alter said, "In the first grade, the children sit and work all day. There's no snack or playtime."

There was nothing for me to say. Sebastian couldn't handle first grade. Point taken.

"So, how is the school search going?" Ms. Banks said.

"I'm calling every autism program on the list of approved private schools, making site visits, and submitting applications," I answered.

Although I had initially been resistant to a completely segregated private school placement, there were two schools I could see Sebastian thriving in. The first, started by a group of parents who'd grown dissatisfied by the lack of options for children on the autistic spectrum, integrated academics and social skills. We passed the application stage and headed to Manhattan for a tour of LearningSpring. After a video presentation, they took Sebastian with a massive group of other applicants to the gym for observation. John and I waited with all the other parents in a separate conference room. It felt just like an audition. Then there was The HeartShare School suggested by Ms. Banks. The school was planning to open a new class in the beginning of April targeting students like Sebastian who were failing in the CTT placement. Designed as a class of twelve, it implemented a variety of methodologies to educate the students using the BOE general education curriculum. They already had four children assigned to the class.

I dismissed any lingering regrets about abandoning inclusion after touring The HeartShare School. Sebastian held my hand, skipping to the car.

"Is this my new school, Mommy?"

"Would you like to come here?"

"Yes."

Everything was lining up. One failed placement didn't have to mean perpetual failure. There was just one more step to achieve. In order to attend either school free of tuition we needed the school team to defer Sebastian's case to the district's central based support team (CBST). LearningSpring would accept tuition from a family while they fought the BOE for funding. We didn't have an extra $90,000, but we could use our home equity to finance a deposit. The HeartShare School, however, would only accept a deferment. With a growing list of grievances and our lawyer, we were sure to be successful.

At the end of February, Veronica's mother was fighting to keep her daughter in Sebastian's class. At her mediation hearing, the precursor to a formal impartial hearing, she sympathized with the teachers, acknowledging that they were dealing with a number of challenging student situations. At that time, the school psychologist replied, "Oh yes, Sebastian. He isn't going to be here much longer."

Veronica's mother reported this to me knowing Ms. Lacking Compassion's breach in confidentiality was a serious violation. My lawyer told me, "We'll hold this in our back pocket if we need it. Don't mention it to anyone right now."

The school psychologist was lucky I had a lawyer. Or perhaps I was lucky. Jail was not a place I cared to end up, but there were all sorts of consequences, natural or otherwise, that I was imagining for this woman. I researched ways to have her certification revoked. In the meantime, I let the information rot in my gut. I could taste the bile every time I had to speak to her. This untrustworthy, rule-breaking, power-wielding witch was a most despicable adversary.

By March, I regained hope that the situation would soon be resolved. We finally had all our private evaluations in hand and a scheduled review with the school team. Every morning on our walk to school Sebastian would say, "Mommy, I need a new school."

"I know, Sebastian. We're almost there."

"Please, Mommy."

"I promise, just a little longer, my love."

I knew it might be difficult to convince the school team to skip the traditional route of BOE placement recommendations, but I had hope. This time John would be at the table, and my friends who worked on public school special education teams assured me that an immediate deferment was possible, especially with all our documentation.

John and I arrived at Sebastian's school for the meeting. The psychologist addressed the teachers, "How is Sebastian doing compared to September?"

Ms. Alter said, "Sebastian is more frustrated, hitting, crying, and threatening to hurt himself. In my opinion, the CTT placement is inappropriate."

The psychologist pulled out our neuropsychologist's report. "My evaluations concur with these findings. We will categorize Sebastian as autistic. I see the neuropsychologist is recommending a class of no more than a 12:1:1 student to teacher ratio. The BOE doesn't have a class of twelve suited for children with autism. Can you ask him to change this recommendation? We have a 6:1:1 class."

Keeping a cool exterior, I rejoiced inside. She had just admitted they did not have a program to meet Sebastian's needs and suggested something as inappropriate as asking an evaluator to change a report to accommodate the BOE. I repeated, "Ask him to change his recommendation?"

"Yes."

Inching my way to helping her justify a deferment, I said, "I think you know about our concerns regarding the autistic programs. Sebastian should not be in a class with nonverbal children on the severe end of the spectrum. He's not that type of child. I'd like to talk about private school options."

Her eyes opened a little wider. "Do you have one in mind?"

We were still waiting to hear from LearningSpring, so I decided to discuss our one sure thing. "We like one that Ms. Alter and Ms. Banks suggested to us."

Looking at the school psychologist, Ms. Banks said, "Yes, you remember the student we had last year who transferred there."

I added, "The school is willing to accept Sebastian in a class opening next month."

She wrote some notes. I looked at Ms. Alter, Ms. Banks, and John, waiting for the deferment.

"I'll transfer Sebastian's case over to District 75. They will offer you a school. You can visit and turn it down. You'll have to do the same with two more placement offers. Then you can go to mediation and an impartial hearing if needed."

Annoyed that I'd allowed myself a moment of hope, I took a deep breath. "That will eat up the rest of the school year. Our case has been open for more than sixty days. Does that help you?" I knew it did. As soon as I wrote that letter to request a para in the principal's office, the BOE legally had sixty days to offer a placement. They wouldn't win at an impartial hearing with that kind of procedural violation.

"No. That helps you. Do you have an advocate?"

"We have a lawyer," I admitted.

"Even better," she said without much feeling.

As my last pitch, I explained, "I'm afraid the remaining spots in The HeartShare School are going to fill up before we get to a hearing."

Ms. Banks turned to the psychologist. "Is there any way to speed up the placement recommendations?"

"No."

Desperate and exposed, I pressed, "Sebastian is miserable. He wants to leave."

She shook her head. "There's nothing I can do."

Ms. Alter added, "We don't want Sebastian to be frustrated, so we're not going to push him to work."

I still didn't have the heart to blame the teachers for the situation. I saw the psychologist as the mason who was responsible for the wall I was now banging my head against. I had never worked with a school psychologist who was unwilling to go out of their way to help a student. I couldn't understand her thought process. The woman who had the nerve to tell my neighbor's mediation team that "Sebastian would be leaving soon" was now barricading a legitimate express lane.

Stress continued to mount. Benjamin's mystery pain returned. It started with a barely noticeable flinch when I lifted him and quickly progressed to piercing outbursts during diaper changes. Blood work and a CAT scan yielded no answers. Benjamin's body was working against him in more ways than one. The October surgery had failed to correct his foot deformity, so we planned for a more aggressive surgical intervention.

Then the LearningSpring's administrator called. "We don't think Sebastian is quite ready for our program at this time." I swallowed hard and squeezed out, "Okay, thank you," hung up the phone, and dropped my head into my hands. I cried so hard I didn't recognize my own voice. The depth of its grief stopped me midstream. I was no stranger to this moment of rejection.

Sixteen years earlier, I stood outside the Limón studio after the audition, expecting rejection but wanting to believe I was worthy and could fulfill my promise to carry Jim's lessons forward. I had done my best, but I couldn't compete with Melora. It was just business, but it felt personal. Melora made it very clear she had no intention to commit to Limón for more than a few months. Other dancers wondered why she even bothered auditioning. I understood. Limón was too tempting an opportunity to give up, but it burned me to see her walking around as if the job were already hers.

One day during the audition process, Melora said to me, "You really have the hard part of dancing down. When you master all the technical aspects, you'll be the whole package." I was speechless, excused myself, and hid in the bathroom. *Don't listen to her, Joanne. Think about the surprise tribute the company members gave you on tour, listing all the things you've done over the last two years, classes you've gotten teachers through by standing in the front of the room, how much they've learned from you. Don't think about how Melora came up to you afterward and said, "I had no idea you've been around so long." Don't let her get inside your head. Oh, my God. They all know there's no hope. The tour and dedication weren't stepping-stones to the company. They were a consolation prize.*

I felt like a fool, a beggar on the street waiting for someone to throw me another dime. My ability to convey a choreographer's intent and emotion through dance couldn't outshine the fact that I didn't have the ballet foundation most other professional dancers had. I never would. No amount of classes would give a twenty-four-year-old, who'd only been dancing for five years, the supple feet and dainty grace of a ballerina.

When the Limón director called and said, "We're going with someone else," I chose to end my dance career. I suppose I could have stood tall, taught my scheduled Limón classes, and waited for the next opportunity to get in, but I was certain rejection would come again. I had to move on. I didn't imagine it would be easy to walk away from something I loved and had dedicated myself to for so long, but I knew I would find the way. I could survive anything after witnessing my father's death, and I trusted God had a new plan for me.

My mother likes to say, "When one door closes, a window will open." She embodies a type of strength I have long sought to emulate. LearningSpring was no longer an option, but at least The HeartShare School wanted Sebastian. It had to be the answer. We waited for the BOE to send us the first placement offer. Four weeks passed and still nothing. Ms. Lacking Compassion insisted the matter was out of her hands.

In April, I called District 75 and discovered the placement officer was on leave. It was pure insanity. We should have gotten a notice within two weeks of Sebastian's review. How many mistakes could they make and still expect us to follow protocol? They asked me to be patient. They had to be kidding. I emailed The HeartShare School to update them on our lack of progress. They gave us their own startling news. The class had opened as planned at the beginning of the month, but now the NY State Education Department wanted them to fill the class by the end of the month. They were actively recruiting new students instead of merely waiting for the CBST to contact them. They had enrolled four more students. Only four spots remained.

I begged Sebastian's teachers to talk to the school psychologist and explain the gravity of the situation. At best, we had three weeks to get a placement offer, visit the school, and formally turn it down. Our lawyer planned to file for a hearing, but that could take another thirty days to schedule.

Three days after I called District 75, we finally received our placement letter in the mail. We made an immediate appointment to tour the suggested public school. Just as we had feared, the students were nonverbal. The program was very well suited for those children, and I was genuinely impressed with what they had to offer. It just wasn't appropriate for Sebastian. I quickly wrote up a three-page document detailing the program's failure to meet Sebastian's needs and emailed it to my lawyer. Later that day, I received another email from The HeartShare School saying there were only two spots left.

Four days later, our lawyer served the BOE with our request for an impartial hearing. She explained that we would first have a resolution meeting before we could schedule a hearing. Although it was not my standard practice, at this stage, I started praying. I could practically hear the second hand on the clock ticking toward the May 7th resolution meeting.

On May 6th, I got word that The HeartShare School had filled the last two spots. It was beyond my comprehension. How was I going to look Sebastian in the eye knowing I had failed to get him the new school he was hoping for?

The following day, I participated in the resolution meeting from my cell phone as I walked home from work. Even though other special ed parents had warned me about the uselessness of resolution meetings, the BOE agreed to defer Sebastian's case to the CBST. For most, private school funding would have been cause for celebration. I was numb. My lawyer didn't have any words of encouragement.

I had been through that list of approved schools a million times. Many were no longer accepting applications, and the rest were too restrictive and depressing to consider. All I felt was a distinct disconnect between my brain and body. I looked up toward heaven for guidance and felt nothing. My previous hardships hadn't built a strong enough foundation to stand up against the tests of motherhood. I couldn't understand why or how I was still breathing. I felt paralyzed as everything I ever aspired to drifted away with the clouds.

The summer after I graduated from Hunter's dance program, I took a month-long Limón workshop in Miami. I choreographed "Waken by Silence" for a composition class. I started the dance as if I were sleeping on my stomach. After several seconds,

I imagined the sound of an intruder breaking into my house and jolted my head up to listen. I froze, staring into blackness. The instructor told the class, "Look at what Joanne is doing. Don't be afraid to be still."

I didn't intend to demonstrate this lesson. I was merely acting out my thoughts of Jim's death and the grief that woke me at night. I wasn't afraid to be still because in dance stillness isn't static. I could take the space without moving my feet. I could feel the energy move from my heart through my arms, fingertips, and out beyond the walls.

When I hung up the phone after the resolution meeting, Sebastian was stuck without an appropriate placement, and I had nothing left to reach for. For the first time, I hated my life.

If You Don't Breathe, You Die

A time to keep, and a time to cast away

I lingered in a state of helpless wanting. If only John and I could step back in time and change the one variable that made the difference. Had we been one toxin, one gene, one month, one hour of conception away from having a normal life? It shouldn't have been out of our reach, but it was. It wasn't the first time I'd struggled with this feeling.

One evening, when Sebastian was a toddler, Benjamin had a seizure. John rushed him upstairs to the bedroom where all his favorite distractions were. In an effort to keep a firm hold on Ben, John, assuming I was watching Sebastian, avoided locking the security stair gate. I wasn't monitoring Sebastian, though, and he crawled up the wooden stairs. As John neared the top of the flight, he spotted Sebastian behind him. John laid Benjamin down on the hall rug and reached out to bring Sebastian to safety. He got within one inch before Sebastian rose up on his feet, lost balance, and tumbled backward to the landing below. John straddled the stairs and two sons grounded in their own miseries.

Then and now, the perfect solution for ensuring everyone's happiness was out of reach. During the months I researched schools for Sebastian, I stumbled upon a public school in

Manhattan with a special inclusion program for students like
Benjamin. I filled out an application, hoping to find an appropriate placement for both boys in the same school.

The school invited Benjamin for an interview and tour. In
the weeks that followed, John and I walked the boys around the
Upper West Side neighborhood attending open houses for tiny
two-bedroom apartments. When we found one, steps away from
the school, I said, "John, can you imagine being able to walk both
boys to school every day? It would be so nice to have that sense
of community."

"It would be worth giving up four bedrooms and a backyard,"
he agreed. When the school rejected Benjamin's application, I
wondered what it would feel like to live in an alternate universe
where my sons were healthy, scholarly, and welcomed.

"John, I'm sorry for getting both of our hopes up. Moving to
Manhattan was such a nice dream."

John shrugged it off easier than I did. "It would have been
nice, but it was just the wrong dream."

Maybe John accepted our life better than I did. Maybe he
didn't care about what the world thought. Maybe he didn't feel
as stuck as I did. Maybe he wasn't dreaming about finding a true
sense of belonging, but I was.

When Sebastian's kindergarten school year came to an end,
I emptied his backpack and flipped through the pages of his
phonics and math books. They were mostly untouched. Kindergarten had been nothing more than a babysitting service. To cap
it all off, his report card affirmed his promotion to first grade. I
was finished trying to understand. Until we found a placement
with an approved private school, Sebastian would, by law, stay
put in the current public school. I couldn't look at that list of
private schools again.

I reached for a new lifeline and turned to the only other
mom I knew who had two children with disabilities. Theresa

had left Brooklyn and moved to West Orange, New Jersey, and she seemed pleased with the educational options for her sons. She worked as an assistant teacher in one of the local schools. She and I had spoken many times that year, and I often joked about moving to New Jersey, but I never seriously considered leaving Brooklyn. We had another lengthy conversation, and I probed her for specific details about what the NJ BOE had to offer. She answered my questions in an effort to humor me. "But Joanne, you'll never leave Brooklyn."

"This time, I'm not so sure," I confessed. Realizing my intentions were shifting, she gave me some contact information and invited me out to tour the area. I didn't know what would be harder, finding a new school in New York or persuading John to move to New Jersey. First, I would have to convince myself. I had always been a proud Brooklynite, but I stood on the island among the wreckage that had been Sebastian's school experience and couldn't imagine what it would take to rebuild.

I contacted the director of special services in West Orange, explained our situation, and detailed the needs of both my children. I could feel her sincere interest, but her answers were carefully constructed. I wondered how many phone calls about hypothetical moves she'd responded to. According to my description, Sebastian was too advanced for their autistic program, so the self-contained Learning and Language Disabilities (LLD) class might be the right placement. The director cautioned that she couldn't make any placement assurances to a nonresident and, without the boys' educational records, she was in no position to promise anything. She did confide that West Orange didn't have a program suitable for Benjamin, so we would have to request a private school or "out of district" placement.

Theresa recommended a private school for Benjamin in a neighboring town. John agreed to accompany me on a tour of the Horizon School, but as expected, he wasn't exactly interested in permanently crossing the river. "Even if we did move, we can't do this for September. There isn't enough time."

"I know it seems impossible, but I'm done." I handed John the twenty-page NYC private school list. "You find a school for Sebastian."

On the day of the Horizon School tour, John and I walked the halls with the principal as she explained all the program's strengths and projected changes. In addition to the standard therapeutic classroom environments, they had a pool and a vision therapy room. A sensory room was under construction. Each student participated in hippotherapy, and there was a fully accessible outdoor playground. They were working to increase technology in the classrooms. Their high school was close by and had equally impressive facilities. It was comforting to know that Benjamin would be able to stay in the same school community until he was twenty-one. In New York, that wasn't the case. As we left the building, John admitted, "I can see Benjamin going to school here."

"Me too. It's a relief to know Benjamin would have a good school option, but it doesn't solve Sebastian's problems. A move has to focus on Sebastian's needs."

Previously, I had made a solo trip to West Orange to observe a K–1 LLD class. The classroom looked like a typical kindergarten room. There were a variety of learning stations and plenty of artwork on the walls. There were desks but also a circle time area with a large rug. The teacher led the class of approximately twelve students in a phonics lesson. I observed a math lesson as well. The children worked first in large groups and then independently for each subject, with assistance tailored according to individual need.

Afterward, the children were led through a movement activity as a transition to a large group story time. It was refreshing to watch an educator who had a gentle yet firm command of her classroom. Behavior issues were addressed immediately to avoid any escalation and to encourage compliance. Expectations and consequences were clearly stated and appropriately enforced. I sat quietly but with the internal giddiness of a child in a toy store. It all seemed too good to be true.

There was no guarantee that the West Orange school district would deem the LLD class as an appropriate placement. I worried that they would recommend an autism program, and we'd be in another fight about placement. I couldn't just pack up my entire family with so little assurance. Could I?

Could I prepare Sebastian for a new school and a new home in two months? He was a child who liked things to be consistent and predictable. He was organized and orderly. He kept his shoes neatly placed on a mat by the front door and his toys perfectly arranged as if on display in a museum. Each item was propped in its exact previous location after use.

What about Benjamin? How could I make him leave the school he loved? The one we had worked so hard to get him into. How could we leave our home in Bay Ridge? Was it physically, emotionally, and financially possible?

Despite my uncertainty, I broke the news to John that I wanted to consider an immediate move to West Orange and convinced him to make a weekend expedition. I studied our finances. It seemed possible to relocate in September if we rented in New Jersey, but that meant managing two houses until we were comfortable enough to sell our Brooklyn home. I would also have to cut my workload significantly to accommodate the commute. My steady work rule is I work only when the boys are in school. I wasn't prepared to start looking for a new job, so we would have to budget carefully and give up date nights.

Leaving New York would increase our medical expenses. The state waived our income because of the severity of Benjamin's disability and gave him Medicaid as a secondary insurance. It paid for diapers and PediaSure. It covered all his co-pays and coinsurance with participating doctors. Benjamin had at least four specialists who routinely cared for him. We were still paying for his non-FDA-approved seizure meds from Canada. His foot orthotics and hand splints needed constant adjustments and eventually replacement. At only nine years old, Benjamin would outgrow his feeding chair, bath chair, car seat, and wheelchair. His last major equipment order cost more than $15,000. I had no idea how our medical expenses would escalate without his secondary insurance. I wasn't even factoring in potential hospitalizations or surgeries. Every 10 percent co-payment would add up. Despite the fact that Benjamin was 100 percent dependent and had a severe seizure disorder, he did not qualify for a waiver program in New Jersey. The state didn't consider him sick enough.

A move terrified me, but I just couldn't risk my sanity any longer. I wanted to gain back a sense of control. My biggest obstacle was getting John to speed up his thought process. He likes to slow cook his decisions. I like to think things through, but I'm much more impulsive. Without John's support, though, I questioned my instincts.

My family had all left Brooklyn and encouraged me to do the same. My brother James kept saying, "Do it already. What are you so afraid of?"

"I don't know. Everything." The truth is, John and I had discussed leaving Brooklyn. We knew selling our first home was just a matter of time. We loved our house with all its detailed woodwork, stained-glass skylights, high ceilings, open floor plan, and center staircase, but we couldn't carve out a space for Benjamin's bedroom and bathroom on the first floor. We didn't want to destroy the beauty and function of the house by installing multiple wheelchair lifts so Benjamin would have full access to the second floor and backyard.

John's family understood the obstacles our home posed, but I doubted they would actively support such a dramatic move. As my sister-in-law Marie stated, "I don't see why something can't be worked out with the school." I didn't have the energy to justify my complete lack of faith in the NYC school system. I continued to strategize a defection I was still frightened to make. It was difficult for me to be out of stride with John. He and I are usually in sync.

Sometimes we all need help in order to view our spouses more objectively. My new specs would come from a longtime friend. Connie had known John longer than I had, but she's like a childhood friend I happened to make in adulthood. Connie's a Brooklyn-born Italian who also lived in New Jersey. She was quick to point out that I had already spent a considerable amount of time contemplating a move, while this was a novel idea for John. Even though we didn't have time to spare, he needed time to process the benefits and consequences. Like it or not, I had to be satisfied with his willingness to take a day trip to the suburbs.

I had grown up one subway stop from Manhattan. When John and I moved to Bay Ridge, it felt like the suburbs to me. Compared to Bay Ridge, West Orange felt like the backwoods, and I had never seen myself as a country girl. I hate bugs. I like to walk everywhere. I'm a good old-fashioned Italian who stares out the window and minds everyone else's business. I enjoy the diversity of Brooklyn and the fact that unity can exist in a borough of over two million people. New Jersey seemed like a collection of towns you drive through where people barely knew their neighbors. Forget about asking for directions. No one knows the name of any streets outside their own tiny radius. I could hardly believe I was considering such change as John and I scoped out real estate offices and collected local rental listings. We stared at each other like a frightened couple on their wedding day. *Should we really do this?*

I wanted the answer to be a clear-cut yes. John hadn't found a school option in NYC, and I wasn't willing to make Sebastian return to that sorry excuse of a school or make two transitions this school year. I was tired of living in a world of bad options. I wanted to be smart enough to solve all our problems. Was running away from home the solution? If we did this, would my reflection be one of failure or perseverance? I remembered having this same feeling the day I realized my dance career was dead.

If you've ever fallen flat on your face and knocked the wind out of yourself, you know how hard it is to get up, ignore the oxygen deprivation, and trust that the spasming diaphragm muscle will relax again. How do you resolve the tension and create a sense of positive movement? Once during center barre warm-ups in class, Jim announced, "Breathe. If you don't breathe, you die." It was so obvious we all laughed, but the message was clear. Breath gives life to an even seemingly static position. I didn't use that lesson to breathe life back into my stagnant dance career. I doubted my ability to breathe life into Sebastian's educational future.

Back in Brooklyn, I walked the streets trying to free myself from the fear of leaving. I never imagined Sebastian would be the reason to drive us out. How had we come to the point where he had no place to fit in? I couldn't get past the feeling that the last two school years had set up a miserable educational foundation. Would he ever be able to build a stable platform? I still believed in his progress, even though my dreams for an inclusive environment had been replaced by the reality that a self-contained classroom would be a better fit. I had also been looking for after-school and social skills programs, but in NYC they were too difficult to find and usually too expensive to consider. Everything felt like a battle, but fear of failure is a powerful anchor.

There is one thing that can challenge fear. Rage.

On an otherwise uneventful day, the four of us went to a local drugstore and ran into some neighbors. The longer we talked, the more overactive Sebastian became. In between my sentences,

I would redirect him. "Don't touch that. Stay over here. Come closer." I got a strong sense someone was watching me. I continued to instruct Sebastian, "Stop jumping. Look at this toy." He managed to escape my field of vision when I took a moment to care for Benjamin, but I quickly found him in the next aisle.

As we continued the conversation with our friends, a woman standing idle on a lengthy checkout line distracted me. Although I never made eye contact with her, she scowled in our direction from time to time. I'd guess she was in her late sixties and wore a spaghetti-strapped white-and-red floral sundress with three-inch red pumps. From behind I'd assume she was a much younger woman. The conflict between my expectations and reality amused me. Surely, she wasn't annoyed at us? I have a habit of being paranoid that I am doing something wrong at any given time. I attribute this to thirteen years of Catholic school.

Sebastian's patience for our shopping expedition had clearly peaked. I took him to the store's vestibule. It was a large open space between two sets of automatic sliding doors where we could see ourselves on the store's security television. This had a calming effect on Sebastian, despite the fact that our presence was frequently activating the automatic doors. As we talked about our images, red pumps huffed by us. Her aggravation toward us was real.

My true Brooklyn spirit boiled to the surface. "What is your problem?"

"You should put him on a leash. My dog is better trained."

A man standing outside handed her a dog leash. I yelled something back, but it didn't make an impact as they calmly proceeded down the street.

I wanted to summon my South Brooklyn warrior and chase her down, but I couldn't leave Sebastian unattended. Still yelling after her, furious that I hadn't thrown the ultimate insult back, I turned to make eye contact with John for his support. He and the long line of customers were staring at me. Their horrified faces snapped me out of my rage. They hadn't heard the exchange. From their point of view, I was experiencing an unprompted breakdown. For Sebastian's entire life I had tried to be the picture of strength my mother had modeled for me, but I was all out of fight.

It was at that very moment I realized Brooklyn was no longer the place to raise my sons. That woman embodied everything I wanted to leave. I wouldn't live in a community that had so little tolerance. My supportive neighbors weren't enough to compensate for our lack of belonging. Like any unhealthy relationship, I had to face the fact that my love affair with Kings County needed to end. I didn't want to be furious in the middle of the vestibule, or frantic in the middle of a major life decision. The doors slid open, and we stepped out.

Part Three

Connecting through
Space *and* Time

12

Process, Not Product

A time to weep, and a time to laugh

Either John loved us enough to make a complete metamorphosis, or my drugstore rage intimidated him. Perhaps since he'd finished his job and was home 24/7, he had time to assess the situation. Maybe it was the combination of all these factors because in mid-August 2008, we signed a one-year lease for a furnished single-family house in West Orange, New Jersey. I'm pretty sure the director of special services in West Orange was surprised when I called her.

"Hi. This is Joanne De Simone. We spoke a few weeks ago about my family possibly relocating from Brooklyn."

"Yes. How are you?"

"I'm well. I just wanted to let you know we'll be West Orange residents on September first."

"Oh? Okay. Hmmm. The registrar's office won't look at the boys until after your move, but I don't want to wait that long to figure out placement. Benjamin is nine years old and needs an out-of-district school, right?"

"Yes."

"Okay, where do you want him to go?"

Really? Where did I want him to go? She approved his private school placement right on the spot, over the phone. West Orange must be a dreamland. With one question she managed to secure Benjamin's educational future and abolish my doubts. When I brought in the boys' paperwork for a preliminary review, they placed Sebastian in an LLD class in our zoned school. I still felt like I was dreaming. We would discuss the rest of the details at their respective upcoming IEP meetings.

The only thing left to do was actually make the move. We had two weeks to pack our absolute necessities, dive off the ruined island, and plant ourselves on the mainland. John and I are well accustomed to the idea of staging. Film sets and dance productions are portable illusions. Props, lighting, costumes, performers, and crew are prepared to change locations. I marveled at the challenge of morphing a studio rehearsal into a full-fledged stage production. The first time you practice on a new stage, everything feels foreign. Magically within a short period of time, I found comfort in the music, the other performers, and the inner desire to reach an audience. It is easier to accept change by identifying and appreciating the things that remain constant. I fed Sebastian a new mantra in an effort to ease all of our anxieties. "Home is wherever we are all together."

We moved on September 1st with some help from our friends Connie and Peter. They mirror our collective sense of organization and efficiency. Knowing we would want all our major necessities unpacked the day of our move, they arrived with manpower and food. By the end of our first night, the kitchen was in a functional state, the boys' bedrooms had a comfortable reminiscence of Brooklyn, and all of our shoes sat neatly lined up on a mat by the front door. The tears I shed driving out of New York that morning had dried. The disconnected feeling from the cut of the cord was fading. The pulse I began to feel was community. At least I hoped so. In every theater, there is a large, dark, unknown presence, the faceless crowd of strangers. They define the level of success. When the music is over, and the house lights are up, the illusion is broken, and the dancer faces the truth with standing ovations or halfhearted applause.

On September 2nd, John and I registered the boys and had a formal meeting with Sebastian's new school team. Sitting in the library, Sebastian spied a miniature Cinderella castle on the top shelf. The team of women adored his love of the fair blonde princess. As he tinkered with the toy, the team accepted his NYC IEP. They explained how we would meet one more time in about thirty days in order to write up a NJ IEP. This would give Sebastian time to acclimate, and the team would continue to assess his needs. He would enter as a kindergarten student because of his late fall birthday. That was fine with me. His previous school year was begging for a little redemption. The meeting ended with a happily-ever-after Disney cliché. Although I didn't want to spoil the moment, I did want a perfectly honest fresh start. I warned his case coordinator, a school psychologist who once lived in Bay Ridge, that Sebastian would likely transition well and in about a month show behavioral challenges.

On September 3rd, I walked Sebastian to his first day of school at Pleasantdale Elementary. We stopped on a corner to wait for the light to change. I caught sight of the street signs. We were on the corner of Pleasant Valley Way and Sunnyside Road. I chuckled, thankful for the literal sign that we had set ourselves on a positive path. I could hear the echoed memories of my brother's support. *Do it already. What are you so afraid of?* It was a sweet-sounding chorus of *I told you so.*

A month later, I met with Sebastian's team to write up a NJ IEP. John was back to work but conferenced in by phone. As I had warned, Sebastian made a wonderful transition but now was growing frustrated and less compliant. I made three suggestions regarding behavioral strategies, but the school psychologist confirmed they'd already implemented such ideas without success.

Then she announced they'd devised a formal behavior plan and wondered if I would approve of it and help to carry it over at home. Oh, Auntie Em, Oz is a fantasy paradise where school teams actually do their jobs without my guidance. Who needs Kansas? I marveled at his new school dream team. Life could be imperfect and yet manageable. Perhaps Sebastian and I would recover from our school phobias.

The schools weren't the only benefit I found for the boys. The town's recreation department had a special after-school program that buddied up children with disabilities and general education students for a variety of sports programs. The goal was to give the children with disabilities access to activities that they might otherwise have difficulty engaging in. The potential life lessons for the general education volunteers were equally valuable. Hopefully, the familiarity between the two groups fosters peer acceptance within the school setting.

It was an ambitious program that resurrected the principles of normalization. I wanted to believe but was skeptical we'd see theory in action. The opportunity came sooner than I imagined, at a Halloween party given at Sebastian's school. Over the years, John had perfected a technique of designing elaborate costumes for Benjamin and his wheelchair. In the school parking lot, I transformed Benjamin's wheelchair into a locomotive.

I wheeled the engineer and his little brother, a soldier from the Nutcracker ballet, into the gym. Sebastian dashed around the familiar environment, comfortable and free. He blended in with the crowd of children. Ever tainted by my assumptions of how others would view him, I scrutinized his behavior for any hint of abnormality. Trying to break my habit of making comparisons, I danced with Benjamin in the back of the auditorium where space was abundant. As he laughed, I noticed a group of teenagers close by.

Teenagers are the breed of children I fear the most. Their unpredictability, overconfidence, and stereotypical obnoxious attitudes make me uncomfortable. I kept an eye on Sebastian running the perimeter of the room, while I choreographed dance moves for the Benjamin Express. Other parents marveled at Benjamin's costume and his contagious glee. He loved the attention. I could see the teens staring, and I just kept moving. A group of two girls and one boy approached us. I held my breath and braced myself.

The boy bent down to talk to Benjamin. I was surprised. People don't usually speak to him first. After a moment, the boy looked directly at me. "What's his name?"

"Benjamin."

"What school does he go to?"

"Horizon."

"Does he talk?"

"No, but he vocalizes."

"My brother is autistic, and he goes to high school with me."

The girls shyly approached to say hello. Benjamin smiled. I watched as the three teens bent down to make eye contact with Benjamin. They had the decency to address him personally as if he was just another kid at the party. After all, that's what he was. He might not have had the ability to break away from my physical guidance, but he'd found liberation on his own. There are days I envy his simplicity. I'm still working on life lessons that come naturally to him.

Knowing we'd found a community that embraced our family, John and I agreed our move was permanent. Making our children's lives better was worth the lousy work commute and selling a house we loved in Bay Ridge. I was relieved the risks paid off, but mostly I was grateful that John and I were standing together on the other side of a trying time. I'm sure he wasn't as ready as I was to make this move, but he did it for us anyway. If he didn't walk away from our marriage then, my bet was he never would. Fifteen years and all our challenges had taught me that being married is a choice we make every day because love is not enough. I love and respect John. He's not perfect. I'm not perfect. Our lives are far from what we'd envisioned, but I wouldn't want to do this life without him.

An unexpected bonus of the move was finding a local, well-respected clinical psychologist who specialized in social skills training. I attended a workshop where he told a "success story" about a young man, an autistic savant type, who couldn't stop talking about air conditioners and grew up to be an air conditioner repairman. I looked around the room at the audience filled with clinical providers smiling and nodding their heads. Apparently, I was the only one depressed by this example.

Although it was a far cry from the image of every cognitively impaired adult I'd witnessed bagging groceries, the story lacked a conversation about this young man's wider personhood. I couldn't help but see him as being unable to break free of the monotony of his obsession. Would he ever have any other interests? Did he have friends? How did he interact with clients, or take instructions from his boss? Was he able to drive to work? If being a repairman made this young man happy, why did it bother me?

I hoped Sebastian would develop a love of something and turn it into a meaningful career. This example fit the bill. However, I wasn't quite sure what Sebastian's interests would be or how they would serve him in the future. He was only five years old. He didn't even know he had autism. Some parents are comfortable discussing disabilities and diagnoses with their children at a young age. John and I didn't feel the need to have the conversation with Sebastian until he seemed cognitively and emotionally able to digest the information.

We hoped he would reach that level of awareness. In my Floortime training, I got the impression that many children on the spectrum don't reach the stage of development that includes "higher-level thinking." While I didn't consider myself to be the type of parent who had unreasonable expectations, I didn't appreciate that this "success story" made me focus on my kindergartener's lifelong limitations. I was hoping the workshop would teach me how to redesign Sebastian's track and create a path that went beyond a typical, expected autism loop.

A few months later, the boys' Brooklyn DOE preschool administrator called and asked me to speak about my parenting experiences with some of her graduate students at a local college. Coming off the social skills workshop where I felt a gap between clinicians and parents, I was hungry to give my perspective to future special educators. After my presentation, one of the students approached me.

"You should write a book."

"Sure. In my spare time," I said, laughing.

"No, really."

She wasn't the first person to suggest my story was worth sharing, but other than writing poems in high school to cope with life and cards for the boys' teachers and therapists, I was not a writer. Two years and a few more college presentations later, I stopped laughing at each student urging me to write the book. Looking for inspiration, I revisited my favorite memoir.

Randy Pausch's *The Last Lecture* read like a good conversation that I never wanted to end. Here was a dying man detailing the lessons he wouldn't live long enough to teach his children. I wanted to document my journey so if I died before Sebastian was cognitively able to understand, he would have something to turn to in order to learn about who I was, why I had done some of the things I did, and what I had discovered. Pausch's stories about the lessons he learned from his childhood football coach drove me to analyze what I'd learned in dance.

I pulled out the boys' photo albums, medical records, and educational files and started writing. The more I wrote about my parenting journey, the more I appreciated how I'd used dance as a parenting tool, from something as obvious as stretching Benjamin when he was an infant, to developing a more abstract idea of introducing ballet to Sebastian as a way to make him conscious of his self-stimulatory movements. Over the next few years of writing workshops and manuscript drafts, dance lessons infiltrated my daily thoughts, and I sought to use these lessons mindfully to manage the conflicts of parenting children with disabilities.

Moving from NYC's imperfect school system and our inaccessible two-story house improved our lives but didn't eliminate the stress. Nothing can, but eight years after we moved to New Jersey, I've found that reaching back to dance lessons gives me a calming perspective and allows me to reframe unresolvable conflicts. I certainly needed better strategies to deal with some old anxieties that resurfaced during Sebastian's middle school years.

Two months into sixth grade, Sebastian initiated a conversation as I tucked him into bed. Referring to a friend's son, he said, "Martin doesn't talk. What does he have? What is it called?"

I looked into Sebastian's brown eyes. *Is this the moment? Is he ready to learn about his disability?*

"He has autism."

"What does that mean?" he asked.

"Well, when you have autism, it can be hard to talk to others and make friends."

He was silent, contemplating this. "Remember when we lived in Brooklyn and I was little? I didn't talk. Do I have autism?"

Relieved that this was happening on a night John was home, I called him in to join us. I smiled at Sebastian and took in this last moment of innocence. I was proud of him for figuring it out on his own and grateful no one at school ever teased or labeled him. As I recapped the conversation for John, I hoped he'd follow my lead and help me find the right words if I stumbled. He gave me a reassuring look. I placed my hand on Sebastian's arm and said, "Yes, you have autism."

Sebastian protested a little, "But I can talk now, and I can read. Can Martin read?"

"I'm pretty sure he reads. Autism doesn't mean you can't learn. You're learning and getting smarter all the time."

"I am getting smarter."

"Of course you are. You just need some help; that's why you're in smaller classes."

"But my classes aren't special."

"Yes, they are," I said, hiding how surprised I felt. On a positive note, it showed the strong sense of belonging and inclusion he experienced at school. On the other hand, how was he so oblivious to his situation and would this news alter the perception he had of himself?

Up until sixth grade, the LLD program had been a good fit for Sebastian, but as the year went on, the curriculum became too challenging. He grew more dependent on his one-to-one aide and yelled at his teachers, insisting they do the work for him. When we sat down for his annual IEP meeting, the teachers agreed his behaviors were born out of his frustration and growing lack of confidence. They were willing to give him additional support so he could continue in the seventh-grade LLD program, but John and I were on the fence about it. In our district, students transition to a new school for sixth grade and then again in seventh grade. With another big change to prepare for, we wanted to consider the idea of taking Sebastian out of the LLD program and moving away from the slower-paced general education curriculum it provided.

At home, Sebastian was so much more independent. While once he was a flight risk, now we could trust him to scooter ride in the park two blocks away by himself. He managed all his personal hygiene and kept his room immaculate. He made sure I followed Benjamin's daily medication schedule. He even played an active role in developing a relationship with his father.

First, by insisting John take him to ballet performances. Then, by taking an interest in movies. Now they go out together every weekend. With so much growth and obvious potential, it killed me that he was falling apart at school.

One of the basic ideas I learned in special education was to meet the child where they are. The curriculum must be sequential, structured, and systematic. A student needs scaffolding until they gain enough skills to remove the support. I'd struggled to teach Sebastian the same basic academic skills year after year. He needed all my attention to complete every homework assignment.

I often joke that Sebastian is smart in all the wrong ways. He learned how to manipulate his teachers and knew how to read them. If he gave the wrong answer on a multiple-choice question, he could see it in their faces and would change his answer. Reading facial expressions and making inferences are skills a child with autism typically struggles with. His abilities have been unbalanced and confusing for as long as I can remember. I always wanted to believe in him, but there were so many nights I found myself yelling at him over math homework. I'd think of my learning disability professors pointing out all the mistakes a parent was making during a recorded homework session. I wasn't yelling at Sebastian because he wasn't able to choose the proper operation or memorize the times tables. I was terrified because if he couldn't complete word problems, how would he ever function in the real world? All those years of homework frustration taught me that I couldn't teach Sebastian something he wasn't ready to learn.

After the IEP meeting, Sebastian's case manager brought John and me to visit a class for children with mild cognitive impairments (MCI). The school social worker showed us some workbooks and told us, "This class doesn't follow the Common Core curriculum. They use spelling and reading comprehension books aligned with the student's developmental level. The math looks more like what you were taught when you were in school."

The last time I observed Sebastian in the LLD math class, he was well-behaved. He took directions from his aide while the other kids were actively working together in groups. He was willing to answer the teacher's questions, but his learning style seemed so passive in comparison to the others. He was a little more vibrant in language arts where he read aloud and answered basic, concrete questions about the text. Even though Sebastian's school team was supportive, and all the uncertainty about where Sebastian belonged was different from our kindergarten experience in Brooklyn, it brought up a lot of old heartache and anger about curriculum driven by standardized tests and the desire to make America's kids smarter than the rest of the world. Children like Sebastian fall further behind every year.

The social worker continued, "This class also works on functional daily skills. So they cook and go on weekly educational trips into the community to practice things like shopping, money management, and communication skills."

As I listened to her, the divide between Sebastian and his typical peers appeared larger than I ever wanted to imagine. "I don't know how I feel about that. John and I already do those types of things with him. John gives Sebastian spare change to practice counting money. We take him shopping and have him pay for items on his own. I don't know if he needs to spend time during the school day to do that."

She replied, "We can certainly talk about individualizing Sebastian's program to exclude the trips."

I didn't doubt a class with experience-based learning would make Sebastian's journey through school much easier. It would also eliminate all the stress his homework caused me, but I didn't want to make a choice based on my life getting easier. I worried that Sebastian's academic bar would drop too low, and I didn't know what it would mean for his future. The future is a parent's forbidden fruit, and I suffer every time I pick it. *Breathe, Joanne. Stay in the present. Focus on the now.*

As John leafed through a vocabulary workbook, I watched the teacher call a student up to her desk. In a hushed tone, she pointed to the child's assignment. "You know this is not your best work. Right?" He nodded. Her gentle but firm approach gave me comfort but shook something within me. I held my breath trying to suppress this unexpected wave of emotion. Too late.

The social worker offered me a tissue. "Did I say something to upset you?"

I shook my head, and the case manager said, "She's relieved."

Is that what I'm feeling? Relief? Sometimes coming to acceptance feels a lot like giving up, but I didn't want to lose faith in Sebastian's abilities, and I didn't want him to lose faith in himself. The teacher hadn't given up all expectations. I was happy about that, but at the same time I was flooded with guilt. We had kept Sebastian in the LLD program exposed to material beyond his independent capabilities, thinking he deserved our belief in him and that down the road it would serve him better. Was it too late to help him build up his confidence and put him on a path of greater independence? Had we set him up to fail? *No, no, Joanne. That's a weight you need to drop, immediately.*

Still wiping tears, I found myself laughing at whatever light-hearted, mood-shifting comments these two women made next, and I knew the case manager was right about my emotions being a sign of relief. In a "Postural Retraining" class at Hunter based on the Alexander Technique, I learned about identifying inefficient movement patterns and how to use my body in a more effortless manner. During a breathing exercise, I lay on the floor and took a deep inhalation. As I exhaled and allowed my voice to stream an unforced tone, my partner rocked my rib cage from side to side, loosening the many tiny, overlooked muscles between my ribs. After repeating the exercise several times, the normally tightened muscles relaxed and signaled a release of energy that the teacher explained is often observed as laughter or crying. I laughed. At first, I was self-conscious, but then a wave of panic came over me because I couldn't stop laughing. My core muscles and ribs tightened, and I ached for a break so I could breathe. When I finally gasped for air, my laughter turned to tears. From one extreme to another, both signaled relief.

The situation with Sebastian wasn't hopeless. We had options. Instead of thinking about where all this was going to take Sebastian, I compared his education to the creative process. When I choreographed dances, I'd first improvise and find steps I wanted to build on. Lengthy movement phrases were born out of these individual steps. Collections of phrases formed, and personal experiences eventually inspired a story or just the emotion I wished to share. All along the way, I didn't know how the dance would look in the end. The end product didn't matter in the heat of the creative process. The only thing that mattered was being present and nurturing the process. I needed to focus on making Sebastian's journey more meaningful, fulfilling, and enjoyable. It was time to show him how to break his negative behavior patterns and teach him to use effective learning strategies.

After discussing it with Sebastian, John and I agreed to switch him into the seventh-grade MCI program and remove his one-to-one aide. The results blew me away. Sebastian did his homework independently. He stopped arguing with his teachers. He set and tracked his own weekly goals. With some help from his case manager, he switched from the special education door-to-door short bus to the general education bus. Then, eager to make friends, he joined the cross-country team.

Sebastian didn't have a strong competitive drive and was content finishing toward the end of the pack, but he loved being a part of the team. When parents would stand on the sidelines cheering him on, he'd smile, wave, and say, "Thank you." While

I'd prompt him, "Look ahead, keep running," I marveled at Sebastian's ability to take in the moment and enjoy the journey without worrying about the end result. Sports, I fantasized, were the key to teaching Sebastian the abstract thinking skills children on the spectrum so often lacked.

When cross-country season ended, and Sebastian announced, "I want to do wrestling," I wasn't convinced my noncompetitive, nonaggressive son was ready for such a fast-thinking, physical contact sport. However, I wouldn't get in the way of Sebastian building on his accomplishments. I did approach the coach and said, "I'm not one of those moms who will insist my child gets time on the mat. There are safety issues, so it's up to you whether or not Sebastian is ready to compete. We're in this for the life lessons." He gave me a confused look and said, "Sebastian comes to practice every day and works hard."

At Sebastian's first wrestling meet, I writhed inside worse than any preperformance jitters I'd experienced as a dancer. I wasn't worried that he'd get hurt or lose. I feared the room full of middle schoolers and their parents watching my son. As Sebastian approached his opponent, I saw his hesitance and lack of core power. *He doesn't know how to use his body. He's not a fast thinker. He's scared, and I don't blame him. This is a rough sport. These kids look tough. He's going to make a fool of himself and won't even know it because embarrassment isn't an emotion he feels yet.*

The referee spoke softly to the pair, and I realized Sebastian's opponent was equally inexperienced. The referee coached the two along. From the crowd a supportive voice yelled, "Good job, Sebastian!" True to his nature, my son dropped his focus and said, "Thank you." While I cringed for a moment, I couldn't help but laugh. The crowd giggled too. Their smiles reassured me they were with him all the way. It's refreshing to witness gratitude in a teenager, especially when they're not in a winning position. *Joanne, remember to focus on all the things that are working well.*

By the end of seventh grade, it was clear Sebastian had not generalized the process-over-product skill he displayed in sports.

"Mom, I want to go back to changing classes."

"What happened when you were in the LLD classes?"

"I was fighting with the teachers."

"Right, because the work was too hard."

"But I'm mature now. That won't happen again."

"You are more mature, and I'm proud of you."

"I know. I know, but I just want to switch classes and have different teachers for math, science, and social studies."

"I understand, but it's more important to be independent and learn how to think for yourself, and now that the work is more appropriate, you've been able to participate in sports. If there's something else you'd like to learn, we can do that outside of school."

I suspected Sebastian didn't really want harder classes but wanted to reconnect with his old classmates. I didn't want him to be disappointed in his capabilities or question my belief in him. I wanted him to know that the quality of his experience is more important than where he ends up.

Even though he didn't fully understand these concepts, the way he'd conducted himself in school and on the field helped me worry a little bit less about his future. My perception of what constitutes a success story had changed. In my early parenting days, I heard it would take years to reach acceptance, but that was a misconception. Acceptance isn't a destination. It's more of a fluid state of being—a dance of balancing the good and bad in every situation.

It's Not about
the Height of the Leg

A time to break down, and a time to build up

Accepting disability is one thing. Dealing with doctors and making complex life-and-death medical decisions is another. During Benjamin's second hospital stay when he was nine months old, a resident interviewed me to collect a medical history. He asked a series of routine questions: "Was your pregnancy full-term? Were there any complications? Was the delivery vaginal? Are you and your husband," he paused, "related?"

"No. We're not," I answered, thinking about my childhood and wild stories about incestuous relationships resulting in abnormal offspring. I had thought all the talk about two-headed babies was just childish, exaggerated lies, but now I faced the fact that people would always judge us, sometimes in ways I couldn't even imagine. So I decided to limit this type of awkward situation with doctors by writing up a detailed medical history to hand over. This solution worked perfectly, especially as Benjamin got older and more medically complicated.

At seventeen years old, Benjamin had had six different doctors. He took three medications for seizures multiple times a day and two nebulized breathing medications to use as needed, plus a prescription for acid reflux. He had lived through sixteen hospitalizations including eight surgeries. The most drawn-out decision John and I tangled with was whether or not to give Benjamin a feeding tube.

The specialist in Chicago first mentioned a feeding tube when Benjamin was one and a half years old. It was obvious to John and me that he didn't need it right then. Subsequent debates weren't as easy. When Benjamin was seven years old, an orthopedic surgeon suggested we place a feeding tube in order to help Benjamin gain weight before his scoliosis surgery. The old statistic from the Chicago doctor rang in my ears: "Fifty percent of children with feeding tubes die in any ten-year period." I didn't want to put Benjamin through surgery in order to have surgery. I was not going to make him live with a feeding tube when he enjoyed eating by mouth. With an Italian heritage, I was determined to fatten him up even if it killed me. After consulting with a nutritionist, I concocted a high-calorie shake to supplement his meals. Benjamin gained plenty of weight and escaped the G-tube.

At twelve years old, Benjamin came down with what the doctors assumed was a virus. He was vomiting for two weeks. No fever. No signs of infection in his blood work. No coughing. No noticeable breathing or oxygenation problems. The doctors encouraged us to wait it out, but Benjamin refused to eat. I'd squirt small amounts of water into his mouth as many times a day as he'd let me, but he grew weak. A vacant look appeared in his eyes. He was a suffering shadow of himself. I kept calling the pediatrician and gastroenterologist, pushing for something more to help Benjamin fight to live. I felt selfish. Part of me wanted him to let go and die. That felt selfish too.

I finally called the GI and said, "I know you wanted to give the increased reflux medication a couple of days, but we're missing something, and I know he's not going to get better." In the ER the doctors tested Benjamin's blood work again and set him up with IV fluids. His physical examination was unremarkable, but to cover all bases they took an abdominal X-ray to check for constipation. It revealed an "opacity" in the right lower lobe of his lung. Benjamin had pneumonia. At least that was their best guess. "Should he see a pulmonologist?" I asked the team of doctors.

"No, that's not necessary," they said. Our pediatrician was skeptical about this diagnosis, but Benjamin improved with IV antibiotics, so I went with it.

From the very start, lissencephaly families had branded my heart with a fear of death by pulmonary complications. Benjamin's abnormal presentation, plus the fact that two pediatricians and an ER doctor didn't hear anything unusual in their examinations, terrified me. Apparently, Benjamin is by nature a shallow breather, which makes it difficult to hear an abnormality that would suggest pneumonia. With the idea that this would be the first of many more bouts of lung infections to come, I wanted answers. What caused this strange form of pneumonia? Should I panic every time he vomits and assume he has pneumonia?

Two months later, I took it upon myself to bring Benjamin to a pulmonary specialist for a follow-up X-ray. Since he was new to us, I provided the pulmonologist with an updated copy of Benjamin's medical history. He flipped through it like an Evelyn Wood speed-reading graduate while shooting questions at me.

"How was your pregnancy?"

"Did you carry full term?"

"Was he born via cesarean?"

"When was he diagnosed?"

"How many times has he been hospitalized?"

"What medications does he take?"

"When did the seizures start?"

It's Not about the Height of the Leg

"Are they under control now?"

He had all the answers to these basic questions in his hands. I was struggling to answer while holding an agitated Benjamin on my lap. I couldn't remember what I had for breakfast, forget trying to remember Benjamin's twelve-year-long seizure history. That's another reason why I had written the medical history. I knew at some point in Benjamin's life, it would become impossible for me to accurately recall years' worth of Benjamin's illnesses, hospitalizations, and medication changes.

Although I was annoyed about the interrogation and my flagging memory, I did what I could to appease the man so I could move on to getting to the bottom of Benjamin's pneumonia.

"How did Benjamin's chest X-ray look today?"

He said, "Fine."

"Good. It's strange to me that he didn't have a cough until after we started treating him for pneumonia. And the coughing hasn't stopped. Our pediatrician has prescribed daily nebulizer treatments."

"Children like Benjamin are at risk for aspiration pneumonia," he said.

"Yes, I know, but this was his only case of pneumonia, and according to my pediatrician and the doctors at the hospital, it wasn't aspiration related."

"In children like Benjamin, it always comes from above," he said, pointing to Benjamin's mouth.

"He had an upper GI in the hospital, and it was fine," I argued.

"I want him to have a swallow study."

It was clear to me that his agenda differed from mine, and he wasn't hearing my concerns, but the fear of Benjamin starting down the road of pulmonary failure outpowered my instinct to find a new physician.

On the day of the swallow study, John and I took Sebastian

and Benjamin to the radiology department at the hospital for the modified barium swallow study. The speech therapist took a look at us and said, "We don't have enough room for all of you in here. Only one person can stay with him." I knew that meant me because Benjamin ate better when I fed him. As John and Sebastian left, I pushed down my separation anxiety brought on by the memories of Benjamin's earliest diagnostic tests when hospital rules forced John out into the waiting rooms.

The speech therapist asked me to place Benjamin into an adaptive feeding seat adjacent to something that resembled a typical X-ray machine. I knew he wasn't going to like sitting in a foreign piece of equipment, and sure enough, he didn't look comfortable when I strapped him in. I provided the speech therapist with a variety of foods to taint with barium. Each food represented a different texture, from pureed to solid. She also put barium in his water and would gradually thicken it.

I stood in front of Benjamin, as directed, with my feet firmly placed inside one floor tile in an effort to stay clear of the equipment. When I tried to feed him, Benjamin lifted his chin, pushed his head back hard against the chair, and cried. I looked at the therapist. "This isn't a good feeding position. It's not how he normally eats."

Unimpressed by my concern, she replied, "Can you hold his head forward?"

She had no idea how strong my son was, and there was no way for me to balance a bowl of food and hold his head in perfect alignment while confining myself to a twelve-inch tile an arm's length away from his mouth. Benjamin continued crying and stuck out his tongue, his sign for "No." Despite his protests, I fed him spoonful after spoonful.

Afterward, I sat with John and the boys in the hallway. Benjamin was calm and comfortable in his stroller. When I offered him some untainted food, he opened his mouth wide.

A few minutes later, I saw the pulmonary doctor wandering around. I assumed he was looking for the speech therapist. I pointed him out to John. "That's not good." In a moment of reversal, I was the pessimist.

"Isn't it typical to see the referring physician come for results?" John asked.

"No. I've never seen a doctor come down to radiology like this. It's a bad sign."

The doctor and therapist approached us in the public corridor. The doctor fired the results at us like the sneeze a stranger on the train forgets to cover, sudden and overpowering. "The test showed silent aspiration across all food textures. Well, we didn't get a clear picture of pureed foods and small solids, but there's aspiration without eliciting any cough. You should go upstairs right now to the GI and schedule surgery for a feeding tube." I looked from the doctor to Benjamin, Sebastian, and John, then up and down the hallway. Why were we doing this here? In a sick haze, I asked, "If he's aspirating liquids, a G-tube will resolve that, but should we worry that he's aspirating saliva?"

His answer was swift. "Then he'll need a trach."

A trach? Kill me now. How did we go from a "fine" post-pneumonia X-ray to a G-tube and a trach?

The child we'd met in Indiana flashed to mind. All the tubes and constant suctioning. The thought of a trach cutting Benjamin's ability to vocalize paralyzed me. I didn't want to live without the sound of his laughter. And how aggressive did we want to be in Benjamin's care? Was I his mother or his nurse? Was I capable? John wouldn't shy away from hands-on medical care, but he was never home. I was the one who would have to deal with all the new equipment, insurance hassles, and school orders. I would be the one to monitor the holes in his stomach and neck.

I protested, "This test wasn't at all representative of how Benjamin typically eats."

Again, he refused to listen to my concerns and said, "Go now and schedule surgery."

John, thinking about more practical matters, added, "What should we do in the meantime, before the surgery? Should we make any feeding modifications?"

He shot back, "No."

I spoke up again. "Shouldn't we plan to take another look at his lungs?"

The doctor's final words to us were, "Just go to the GI, now."

Benjamin's swallow study results shocked the GI. "He's been eating fine all this time." After consulting with the pulmonologist, the GI suggested we go ahead with the G-tube surgery, but he also told us, "This isn't an emergency," so we took it as a halfhearted recommendation. We spent the next two weeks running tests that, to our relief, ruled out the need for a trach. Still, John and I felt ambivalent about the G-tube.

We gathered all the test results and consulted with Benjamin's pediatrician. Dr. Gabriel spread the papers across his desk. "Benjamin has had oral motor problems for his entire life. I still don't think he had pneumonia, but even if he did, it's not time for surgery. This is a quality of life issue. How is he eating?"

John spoke first. "He still loves eating by mouth."

Dr. Gabriel continued, "Don't disregard Benjamin's pleasure. Some doctors look at a child like Benjamin and make assumptions about what they need."

A big part of me was glad he wasn't advocating for surgery, but I wanted to look Benjamin in the eye without regret. "Dr. Gabriel, if we don't do the surgery and Benjamin comes down with another case of pneumonia, I'm going to feel like it's my fault."

"Pneumonia can be treated with antibiotics, and yes, repeated pneumonias would warrant intervention. But we're not there yet. If you want, I can refer you to a colleague for a second surgical opinion."

It's Not about the Height of the Leg

I didn't want to complicate the matter with one more voice. Sometimes a second opinion fills a void that one doctor can't fill. John and I have had that experience where we wanted a better rapport with a doctor or were seeking out someone with a more favorable surgical technique. A second opinion would only serve to justify our own conclusions. We didn't need that. We needed to come to terms with our true feelings based on our observations of Benjamin. We needed to push aside the well-intended pressures placed by the doctors. We had to look past the assumptions made by some professionals regarding children like Benjamin. After all, the specialist in Chicago had told us Benjamin needed a G-tube when he was a year and a half. Clearly, that wasn't the case. It is tempting to group our son into a neat statistic, but as a family, we still maintained the right to keep him out of this numerical box.

Even though Benjamin wasn't capable of making major life decisions, he was in a partnership with us. We tried every day to listen to his nonverbal cues. He was showing us that he still wanted to eat. Unlike his behavior during the modified swallow study test, at home he was able to cough and clear his airway during meals. The upper GI series completed during his pneumonia hospitalization showed "normal esophageal motility." Food made him happy. Eating is a social activity. I allowed the frightful picture painted by the swallow study to fall out of focus, and John and I gradually reduced and then eliminated our conversations about surgery. Life gave us imperfect options, and our lack of action spoke to me. In special education, we believe sometimes less is more because too much intervention can be overwhelming and unproductive.

Two years later, after a simple upper respiratory infection followed by a case of the flu, Benjamin lost nine pounds. At that time, his orthopedic surgeon recommended surgery to stabilize Benjamin's dislocating hip and pushed for us to consider a feeding tube.

"Benjamin needs to gain weight before we can do this surgery. A feeding tube will improve everyone's quality of life. It will be easier for you to regulate calories. Additional weight gain will improve his overall health. It will be easier for others to take care of him in the future. Why are parents so conflicted about feeding tubes? Benjamin will be the same child."

I agreed with all these statements, but I didn't want Benjamin to need a feeding tube. It's foreign, unnatural, and that state of being already held us captive. It would be a visual reminder of his dependence, as if everything else weren't reminder enough. It would scar his flesh, the belly I kissed when he was a baby. It threatens a familial social bonding activity, and we have so few of those. It would move us even further away from normal, and a part of me will always feel denied.

Every invasive procedure scars my soul and threatens my humanity, my place as Benjamin's mother. Every time a doctor needs to intervene, my fears build like a tsunami after an earthquake. In order to give my son up to a doctor, I have to push myself under the wave. I'm always in a state of drowning. Drowning my motherhood.

One of Benjamin's doctors suggested that parents harbor guilt about feeding tubes because we feel as if we've failed to sufficiently nourish our child. It's a reasonable explanation, but guilt is so much more complicated for parents like me. When Benjamin is suffering, I feel guilty for giving him this life, and, with every intervention, for giving him the means to survive it.

John and I tried to gauge Benjamin's vitality. We looked into the future, when Benjamin might no longer be with us, and we asked ourselves, "What is the right choice? If he doesn't wake up tomorrow, will we still be able to sleep at night?"

John often analyzes situations based on math. "He lost nine pounds. That's about twenty percent of his body weight, and we've struggled to keep him over fifty pounds for a long time. I think it makes sense to do it now."

I broke down my reservations by using dance to build a new perspective. *There Is a Time* taught me that a quality performance does not depend on perfect technique or some idealized version of a dancer's body line. It's not about how high you can lift your leg. The goal is to be so pure of intent that you become transparent to the point of existing beyond yourself. The artist should not distract the audience and prevent them from engaging with the dance. The message of the dance is the main character, free to reach the viewer.

Benjamin, at fourteen years old and forty-three pounds, would never regain enough weight for hip surgery without a G-tube. He still enjoyed eating by mouth, but he'd regressed to smaller portions of pureed foods. I still hated the idea of placing a hole in my son's stomach, but this wasn't about me. It didn't really matter what I wanted. The decision had to be based on Benjamin's needs, and he needed me to remove myself from the narrative.

A couple of days after the G-tube surgery, a gastroenterologist we didn't know stopped by Benjamin's hospital room. We had cluttered the place with stacks of Benjamin's favorite books, stuffed toys, and DVDs. John, my mother, and Sebastian sat next to the bed as I greeted the doctor. He shook my hand, looked at Benjamin, and asked, "Does he live at home? With you?" I processed this odd first question, wondering why it mattered.

"Yes, he does," I said. Part of me thought, *Check his chart. The seven-page history I wrote is in there. Yes, my son has a lot of complex medical needs, but take a look at us. We are a family, as valid as any other.* The other part of me accepted the complicated dance of doctors, patients, and parents.

Accepting this life doesn't make all the conflicts go away. One document on Benjamin's medical history can't answer all of a doctor's questions. An entire book can't give the whole story. The toughest question Diana, my friend from the Brooklyn DOE, asked me to address with her college students was, "What are one or two things you really want them to know?" I believe my answer applies to teachers and doctors. The way I see it, they both work from a disadvantaged starting point. When it comes to understanding families, they rely heavily on what a parent is willing to divulge. No matter how much information they have, they still can't assume to know what it is to be that parent. The full picture is always out of reach. It's normal for human beings to judge; just resist allowing those judgments to guide how you treat others. If Diana asked me this question today, I would expand further about the art of acceptance.

After we moved to New Jersey, John and I brought Benjamin to a new neurologist. One of our friends described him as "a genius with seizure medications." As I discussed the details of Benjamin's history, I felt an old sorrow resurfacing. We still had so many of the same unanswered questions. "Our previous neurologist didn't find a genetic cause. Could this have been from a fever I had the week I conceived? Or a virus? Or the chemicals my next-door neighbors used while renovating their house? Or lead in our drinking water?" I paused to suppress a volcanic surge of emotions. How was I still blaming myself? Dr. Devinsky folded his hands and took a deep breath. "We're just not smart enough yet to know why this happens."

His honest, even vulnerable answer gave me clarity and peace. There was no need to blame myself for Benjamin's rare neuronal migration disorder, or my inability to solve a mystery numerous gifted medical minds had not been able to conquer. Parents, like children, learn when they are ready.

14

Live in the High Space

A time to love, and a time to hate

Very few are privy to all that it takes for a dancer to arrive onstage—the bloodied feet, months of rehearsals, and self-doubt. An audience receives the polished version. It's never as easy or as glamorous as it looks. One Father's Day weekend, Sebastian and I had planned to take John out, but our sitter canceled, so we settled for a movie night at home. John dimmed the lights, and all four of us relaxed in front of the TV. Benjamin's head snapped back. I knew he was about to go into a "vomit seizure." His eyes rolled upward, and he didn't look at me when I called his name.

After seventeen years of managing seizures, I'll admit, we'd habituated. It's what I like to call an unreasonable norm. Benjamin has several different types of seizures daily despite the use of three anticonvulsants. His ability to laugh at his favorite music or TV show during seizures suggests Benjamin's habituation too. We ride out the majority of these episodes knowing they will be brief, but vomit seizures are different. They can last for hours and put Benjamin at risk for aspiration pneumonia.

I rushed for his emergency rectal Valium. John covered Benjamin's bed with waterproof pads and laid him down on his side. He vomited all over himself as I administered the dose. He fell asleep before I could change his clothes. I'd learned the hard way not to disturb Benjamin while the Valium is working. He'd just throw up again.

It was 10:19 p.m. John and I took turns checking on Benjamin. Every time I returned from Benjamin's room, Sebastian would look at me through the darkness. Whenever there's uncertainty around Benjamin, Sebastian reacts with nervous anticipation. I stand between my two sons, measuring their emotional weight and the forces surrounding them, and seek a balance.

"Benjamin just needs to sleep. He's okay," I said.

It's like being onstage just before the lights come up. Space is a living partner. Sometimes it's uncomfortably tangible. When it's too dark to see, you have to find a comfortable breathing rhythm and trust the light will come.

Benjamin does well with Valium. He sleeps for a few hours and often wakes up as if nothing has happened. The vomit seizure tends to be a bit unpredictable. When they started, the neurologist didn't agree they were seizures. I thought our debate would come to an end when Benjamin experienced one during a routine EEG, but it didn't. There was no clinical finding, but I later learned EEGs don't register seizures in the deeper parts of the brain. The GI ran several tests and ruled out other possible causes. The only thing that stopped the episodes was the Valium, so the GI concluded it was a seizure. Even with the Valium, we have to wait it out and monitor his breathing. Seizures and Valium could cause Benjamin to stop breathing.

I have only called 911 once after administering Valium. Benjamin was breathing fine, but he vomited blood. I wanted to make sure he didn't bleed to death from an unknown internal injury.

"Does he typically make eye contact?" the emergency room doctor questioned.

I explained, "The Valium is making him sleepy. He's usually quite interactive." The doctor shot me a skeptical look. I find it curious that people assume a child with multiple disabilities would naturally present as disconnected and unaware. When the medication wore off and Benjamin woke, I played his favorite music. He laughed, kicked his legs, and took turns vocalizing with me. The doctor's face lit up in surprise.

Now as I looked at Benjamin's face, I could see a crease between his eyebrows. John and I took turns watching Benjamin through the night. At 5:45 a.m., Benjamin woke up seizing and vomiting. He was able to look at me when I called him. Unwilling to give him more Valium in less than a twenty-four-hour period without calling 911, we followed tried-and-true strategies consistent with the less aggressive, more care-and-comfort approach the doctor in Chicago had discussed with us so many years ago.

When Benjamin was small, we noticed certain seizures would fade if we stimulated his senses. We sang, danced, played TV shows, encouraged him to vocalize, or gave him a shower. Desperate to clean the vomit off him, I asked, "Benjamin, do you want a shower?" He looked at me. "Okay, let's get a shower, beauty." Keeping him on his side, I fought his stiff limbs and peeled off his vomit-soaked clothes.

Benjamin loves the sound of running water. I refer to a shower as laugh therapy. I swear it helps to keep his lungs clear. Under the spray of the shower, I saw Benjamin's eyes focusing on me again. "Do you want to hear some music?" He smiled and widened his eyes, a sure sign he was with me. He vocalized as I sang one of his favorite songs, "Moon, Moon, Moon," by Laurie Berkner. He vocalized in response, but his left leg was kicking from time to time. Although I was sure that was a sign of seizure activity, I thought we might be past the vomit stage. After a good half hour, John carried Benjamin into his room. Sometimes just laying him down can start the cycle again, so John held Benjamin upright on his lap while I dressed him. Once he was sitting up watching his favorite DVD, I hoped we were in the clear.

We weren't. He threw up again and then went to sleep. I looked at John. "The Valium is still in his system. Maybe he just needs to sleep. Let's hope his brain resets."

When Sebastian woke, the first words out of his mouth were, "I didn't hear Benjamin last night."

"He slept through the night," I said.

Then he noticed Benjamin's shower chair set up in the bathroom. "You gave him a shower? He threw up?"

"Yes," I said, "he's sleeping now. Let's have breakfast."

An hour later, we heard Benjamin laughing at the TV.

I ran in to celebrate with him. "Hey, Benjamin. You look so much better. Is this show good?"

After five minutes of acting out an episode of *Teletubbies* I can perform in my sleep, Benjamin threw his arms outward. A typical morning seizure then morphed back to vomiting.

"That's not fair to you, Benjamin."

He didn't have much left in his stomach. I checked his oxygen level for the bazillionth time. I slowly pushed his morning seizure med through the G-tube, hoping it would stay down at least twenty minutes. Years earlier I had been instructed by his neuro not to repeat a dose if it stayed down that long. At the twenty-minute mark, he spit up a small amount. "Can't re-dose you now, buddy. Let's hope you got enough to help."

Sebastian stood in the doorway. "Is he okay?"

I waved my hand, signaling him to head toward the kitchen, and tiptoed out after him.

"Benjamin's not better yet. I want him to sleep some more. You want to go for a bike ride?"

"Sure."

John and I watched Sebastian ride off.

"Do you think other parents would just head to the ER?" I said. "We've seen this seizure pattern before."

"What do you think they'd do for him?" he asked.

"If they considered this a status situation, they'd push more emergency meds. I've seen kids on the Facebook support group end up on life support due to the amount of meds it takes to stop the seizures. Is that what he needs? Do we want to put him through that?"

John shook his head. "He's already sleeping. Let's see how he wakes up."

I passed the time with one eye on Benjamin and another on my Find My iPhone app tracking Sebastian in the park up the block.

Two hours later, Benjamin woke up without any startles, vomiting, eye rolls, or repetitive leg movements.

"Benjamin, that's no way to wish your father a Happy Father's Day. Don't be bad," I teased as I kneeled by his side.

He smiled at me.

"Don't you laugh at me." He laughed hard. I don't know why these particular phrases crack him up, but I love his sense of humor.

I yelled out to John, "Daddy, he's trying to kill me!"

John joked with Benjamin, "Bad kid." We all laughed together.

John's demeanor shifted. "Good thing we didn't go out last night. What if that happened with the sitter?"

"I know. It would have sucked, but we never go far. She's dealt with poop and vomit before. She knows the Valium drill."

When Sebastian came home, he paced around, debating his choice of words. "I wish it wasn't so hard to take care of Benjamin."

"Me too, buddy. It's okay to feel that way, but this is the way he was born, and we love Benjamin."

John added, "We're doing the best we can to take care of him."

While there were other things that could have been said about Benjamin and imagining things from his perspective, I could tell by Sebastian's silence he was thinking about something else.

"Ms. Rose told me sometimes friends change," he said.

Ms. Rose, his school social skills counselor, had been teaching Sebastian about the difference between an acquaintance and a friend because a student who regularly waved to him a year ago no longer did.

"He was my friend last year."

"Sebastian, if someone waves at you, it doesn't make them a friend."

I'd been telling him this for the past five years, but the lesson hadn't stuck, so I tried a different approach.

"Remember I told you about my childhood best friend? We really didn't talk much after we went to different high schools."

"I know it's tough to understand," John said. "People change and so do friendships. It's all a part of growing up."

Sebastian seemed content knowing everyone experiences the same thing. He's grown so much. A year earlier, he would hide in the car in the garage every time Benjamin cried. Now he hovers, while saying, "I'm fine." We can trust him to ride in the park alone, and he calls us from his cell phone at predetermined times. I only wish he could make true friends because he so desperately wants to. His middle school peers are kind. They talk to him in school, cheer him on in after-school sports, and accept our invitations to movies, but they don't call him on their own. I love that Sebastian still holds my hand when we walk down the street and says, "I love you" in public, but a thirteen-year-old boy should have a friend to talk to about girls and complain about his parents.

Just when I thought this little therapy session was over, Sebastian's eyes welled up.

"I need a hug."

"Sure," I said, moving closer.

"Will all my friends decide not to be my friends?"

My heart fell, but it was great that he was able to digest this idea and think about it in a larger context. It gave me hope that he would keep moving forward toward living happily without us one day. "No. That's not going to happen."

"I wish I wasn't autistic. It would be easier to make friends."

I held him tight and took a deep breath, hoping he'd do the same. Pain has a way of making your body feel smaller. Breathing into the areas that hurt relaxes the muscles and gives the body the freedom to expand.

"It's okay to feel that way, but you're a great kid, Seb."

John added, "Think of all the new kids you've met this year."

My greatest challenge has been watching Sebastian as he tries to figure out who he is and how he belongs. I'm not a passive person. I'd rather be onstage than waiting in the wings. It's hard to be on this journey, but I've learned not to fight it even when his struggles bring me down. Gravity is a force modern dancers use to generate movement. Fall and recovery is a normal sequence in nature and a fundamental element in the Limón technique.

A fall does not have to result in a collapsed state of being. This is where oppositional forces come into action. When you fall, you choose a part of the body to act as the high point from which you will suspend. Limón teachers describe the body as having a plumb line extending infinitely upward. When you're standing, it's easy to imagine the spine as that line, with your head being the high point. If you drop your head, the suspension point shifts to the next-highest point of your spine. The plumb line is not limited to the spine. If you bend sideways, the high point will be somewhere in your ribs.

Jim would demonstrate fall and recovery by swinging his arms up across his chest, releasing them down and out to his sides, and allowing the momentum to take them up until his hands, eyes, and chest would naturally reach toward heaven. He'd linger there, suspended long enough for you to believe he could actually see God.

"Live in the high space," he'd say. Living in the high space was equally divine to witness and experience.

Imagine the movement of a swing. Release any resistance and ride the natural path to suspension. The feeling of clarity and ease is short but memorable. The drop that follows is not a force drawing you away from the previous wonderful moment. It is the momentum that will bring you up to the next suspension if you let it.

The common mistake is to try to shortchange the fall, and power your way up to the top. But fulfilling the goal of weightlessness has little to do with how hard you try. You must release your resistance and trust you can follow the natural path that will lead you to an effortless state of contentment.

I struggle imagining Benjamin's and Sebastian's futures. While parenting and my teaching career have taught me that a diagnosis does not define a child, separating who my sons are from their disabilities is difficult. Not because I'm stuck focusing on their challenges—I see Benjamin's ability to smile in the face of pain and Sebastian's growing capability to empathize during hyperstimulating experiences. I'm proud of them both, but the world will always categorize them, and I don't want other people's perceptions to negatively alter how they see themselves.

I find that people who buy into stereotypes think they have a complete understanding of a particular community. I see this even among the many professionals the boys have brought into our lives. Doctors, teachers, and therapists all have opinions about kids with autism or CP. There's a great variation in how close their knowledge brings them to the truth. An audience cannot move through your space and your time as you do. A performance can affect the audience, but they can't live in it, no matter how close they are to the stage. Every seat in a theater has a slightly different view. Each individual in those seats uses their knowledge, instinct, and common sense to make interpretations.

It is the combination of all these qualities that determines perspective. That is why comprehending even the simplest forms of art and life is so uniquely complicated. Performers strive to reach everyone but cannot control how an audience perceives them.

I often hear parents say they are grateful for their children's disabilities and wouldn't change them for the world. While it's true that Benjamin and Sebastian have made me a better person and a better educator, I could have lived without acquiring such growth. If we play the hypothetical game, I would have changed everything in order to spare them. I love my boys for who they are but hate the challenges their disabilities give them.

One of the most intimate sections in *There Is a Time* is "A Time to Heal." Jim was teaching the choreography in an effort to cast the duet. During rehearsal he asked me to partner with him. He lay on the floor wounded. Kneeling beside him and placing my ear next to his heart, I breathed slow deep breaths. With each of my inhalations Jim raised his chest and with each exhalation we lowered down in unison, one desperate soul breathing life into another. I gathered his body into a sitting fetal position. I rocked him in this embrace, like an infant in a cradle. In the dance there was an ability to heal. A year later, Jim was dead. I mourned the destroyed fantasy of having such power, but I vowed to continue learning from his lessons and to look for him in the high space. When I left dance, I harbored a deep guilt for letting his lessons die.

I spent the first ten years of motherhood believing I'd failed my children. I looked at my journey from dance to special education as some bizarre cosmic mistake that led me to having two children with disabilities, and if I'd only stayed committed to dance, it all wouldn't have happened. Now that I've allowed myself to think about the skills I gained as a dancer and have worked to generalize those skills, I can see the building blocks life gave me, and I am whole. Losing my love for the world of dance drove me to special education. Sebastian's failed school placements led us to New Jersey. The move helped drive me toward acceptance and, as a family, to accomplish a sense of belonging. When life knocks me down, I will strive to fall with the direct intention to rise.

The high space is more than just a suspension after a fall. I first discovered a concurrent light freedom and secure groundedness while performing a simple warm-up combination in Jim's class. Standing straight with my arms reaching up and rising on the balls of parallel feet, I found an effortless balance. I sensed that every part of my body was reaching out to something far beyond. All of my energy was committed to that one thought, and that is when I felt it. My feet were to the earth, my hands to the sky, and my soul hanging in between.

In life, there's always a high space, and it is limitless.

15

Surrender

*A time to embrace, and a time
to refrain from embracing*

At Hunter, prior to every performance, the dance company would gather for a class led by one of our professors. One evening, Professor David Capps instructed us to lie on the floor with our eyes closed. Jim's directives filled my head: *Don't try to change anything. Just notice.*

David began, "Allow the floor to support you. Forget about what happened earlier today. Put all thoughts out of your mind. Sink into the floor. Imagine the walls one level down coming up to the floor to support you. Imagine the foundation of this building reaching up through the walls and the floor to support you. The subway is reaching through the foundation, the walls, and the floor to support you. Beneath the subway, see through the layers of the earth. The core of the earth is sending energy through each layer, into the subway, through the foundation, the walls, and into the floor to support you." Maybe it was the power of suggestion, but my body released into the floor. Every bone and achy muscle felt supported.

I opened my eyes and focused on the windows lining the front wall of the studio. The long frames of glass peaked high above, like church windows, but without the colorful pictures of saints. The studio was my church preparing me to perform. I was a small but necessary part of a larger whole ready to surrender to all the joys and mishaps that awaited me onstage.

Dancers use their senses, hearts, and instincts to analyze everything around them. I tuned into this ability at a young age. The day before my father died, I asked him, "Daddy, who's going to write the will, you or Mommy?"

Without a moment of thought, he answered, "Mommy." I was a nine-year-old preoccupied with material possessions, but I thought I caused my father's death or somehow knew it was going to happen. I labeled myself a clairvoyant after listening to all the stories about my Italian elders having meaningful visions of dead family members.

It was my mother's screams that woke me during the dark morning hours. "Joooohnny, Joooohnny, Joooohnny!" My senses fired up. I pushed through fear and my parents' doorway. I can't remember who was trying to block me, but through a web of arms I saw my brother performing CPR on my father's lifeless body. Neighbors and the firemen from across the street gathered and escorted me out to the hallway. On my way down the narrow staircase, I squeezed past one of our parish priests on his way up. I knew why a priest would be there.

Assuming my mother would also die, I attempted to save myself from another surprise loss by putting myself to sleep every night with frightful fairy tales made up of every imaginable death scenario. From time to time, I'd try to imagine Benjamin's last day. Would I get a call from the school nurse? Would he simply pass during the night? Would he slowly fade before our eyes? When Benjamin was a baby, I could visualize him as a happy, completely dependent twenty-year-old. Now I looked at my seventeen-year-old son, and I couldn't imagine him growing older. I didn't know if that's because he looked like a prepubescent boy and wouldn't live long enough to grow a beard, or if I'd end up dying before he needed a shave.

Except for the geneticist who told us Benjamin had a 50 percent chance of living until ten years old because of his need for a feeding tube, our doctors haven't mentioned life expectancy. Lissencephaly taught me that underdeveloped brains struggle to manage growing bodies. At some point the ability to fight repeated bouts of pneumonia and seizures wanes. Medication and interventions, like feeding tubes and tracheostomies, can extend life but cannot change my son's nature. Most children with lissencephaly die young. I have spent Benjamin's entire lifetime mourning the deaths of children I've met on the Internet.

Sometimes, after yet another obituary notice appears in my lissencephaly Facebook group, I walk around Benjamin's room looking at his framed Raymond Briggs's *The Snowman* poster, Beatles' "Yellow Submarine" snow globe, and *Where the Wild Things Are* plush toys. I see Benjamin smiling at these things. I hear his laughter as John reads *The Big Red Barn* for the twelve billionth time. When Benjamin dies, will we leave his room frozen in time or pack everything away? Will I avoid his favorite song, "Sweet Baby James"? Will the words from *Goodnight Moon* torture me every evening when I lie in bed? Will I feel relieved or lost without the doctors' appointments, the medication, feeding, and diaper schedules? How will I get through the day when Benjamin's smile and laughter live only in my imagination? I'm not sure how parents move on after their kids die, but I'm terrified by stories of children like Benjamin celebrating their thirtieth birthdays.

Benjamin's doctors don't have crystal balls, and death goes unspoken. I won't put them in the awkward position of attempting to slap an expiration date on Benjamin. As a teacher, I know how it feels to have a parent look me in the eyes and ask, "Will they be okay?" and have no reliable answer. After seventeen years, I worried less about Benjamin dying and more about him surviving beyond John and me. When we're gone, who would look beyond Benjamin's scars and see his brilliance?

John and I visited a residential school when Benjamin was eleven years old. The administrator encouraged us to put Benjamin's name on the waiting list. He said, "You have to think of everyone's quality of life." The white cinder block bedrooms had an institutional feel. In the cafeteria, the number of students in wheelchairs outnumbered the staff. Children sat silently waiting for help and attention. If orphaned, Benjamin would need to live in some kind of medical facility. We had named guardians in our wills, but no one in our family could dedicate their life to the type of care Benjamin requires. Hospitals are not homes. I pictured my son hooked up to tubes, nothing more than an insignificant number on a chart. With that in mind, I'd rather bury him than leave him behind.

We cannot protect Benjamin from the havoc nature imposes on him. Our only goal is to give him the best possible quality of life. The definition of "quality" has always been hazy, dependent on Benjamin's needs and our capabilities. Dr. Fifty Percent drew a parenting line with aggressive treatment on one side and care and comfort on the other, but how hard can we or should we fight Benjamin's nature? And at what cost? How many machines should one child rely on to live? What is Benjamin's threshold? What is mine? What is John's? Do we matter in this equation? How will we know when Benjamin has had enough? Will we recognize the time when Benjamin declines to the point of not being Benjamin and let nature take its course? As my brother James says, "Every day brings us one step closer to death."

A few years ago, a bright and talented eleven-year-old boy in my community died in a car accident. He was a stranger to me, but I wept for his family. At the time, I wondered why this child, and not mine? Of course, now I realize how ableist my thoughts can be. As I see it, society is fond of creating hierarchies and placing one type of intelligence at the top. We are conditioned from the start to celebrate good health, good grades, and good behavior. When we birth children who don't have these traits, we grieve because our culture always told us to, and we anticipate a societal outcasting. Eventually, we realize our grief has more to do with the world's attitudes and less to do with our children. We learn we've probably supported the ableist ideology through thoughts and actions, and then we must balance the dissonance created by this realization. I will spend the rest of my life checking myself for ableist thoughts, but I won't crucify myself for coming to this realization late in my journey.

In special education, it's common practice to validate a child's feelings. I believe it's equally important to validate a parent's feelings, no matter how shocking they may seem. I once worked with a parent who thought using a female baby doll during speech therapy would encourage her son to grow into a "cross-dressing homosexual." No matter what I said, I couldn't convince her otherwise. I advised her to speak directly with the speech therapist, but her fears bothered me.

After a day of banging my head against an ideological wall, I started to see things differently. This was her son. She lived with a great deal of stress. My opinion didn't matter, and it wasn't my job to change her beliefs or dismiss her fears.

I'm comfortable accepting my feelings no matter how conflicted they are because I redefined parenthood long ago, and now dance supports my instinct to embrace the range of emotions that arise in each situation. While our friends' children are giving valedictorian speeches, going off to college, and getting married, I drift between Benjamin's smile and the image of his name on a headstone. The future will take care of itself. Right now, it's my job to prepare Benjamin and Sebastian to live life without me, even though their needs and capabilities are so different.

How do I leave a medically complex child in the hands of strangers when he cannot advocate for himself? Sebastian will hopefully continue to gain independence and enough social skills to form relationships that can replace our bond. One of my greatest accomplishments in life is giving my autistic son the ability to truly sense the power of love, and yet I know that one day, this gift will allow me to break his heart the way my father's death broke mine.

Today I'm thinking about everyone's quality of life. Both my sons deserve to live at home like any other child. Yes, it would be nice if Benjamin's disabilities didn't place limits on my ability to work, strain my marriage, or divert my focus from Sebastian's needs, but this is the family we are. It does me no good to fantasize about it being any other way, but acceptance is a fluid dance.

For as long as John and I are capable, Benjamin will remain a part of a community outside of people who are obligated to him because of a paycheck. I will grow old, probably prematurely, watching Benjamin's decline. Even on Benjamin's most resilient days, there's a corner of my mind lingering backstage in darkness with nervous anticipation, aware of the divide between my original dreams of motherhood and reality. All parents have stress, but the parents I know who have children with disabilities have perpetual traumatic stressors. As my friend Doreen likes to say, "It just never stops. Not until they shut the lid."

It's no surprise that I've been overly preoccupied with death from a young age. Every evening, I think of my demise in practical terms. If I were to have a heart attack or stroke, my only wish is that it happens after I administer Benjamin's final round of medication. That way, he'll have a better chance of avoiding a fatal seizure by the time John gets home from work in the wee hours of the morning. I take some comfort in knowing that at this stage Sebastian might do the right thing and call for help. I test him often: "What do you do if Mommy falls down, and you can't wake me?"

One of the ways teachers try to reduce students' anxieties is by following predictable schedules. As a dancer, I had specific daily warm-up and preperformance rituals. Today, Benjamin and I perform a sacred bedtime routine. It's difficult for me to lift Benjamin from his favorite chair, which sits one foot off the floor. We don't own a bulky mechanical lift system, so I created the next best thing. Years of spotting children as a gymnastics instructor taught me how to use my whole body to support weight. I strap a medical-grade patient lifting belt through the loops of the transfer mat used to line Benjamin's chair. I slide my head and right arm through the loop and cradle my son. Before I stand up, I think of the dance directives that will allow me to use my body efficiently and without pain. *Bend and send your knees over your second toes, drop your pelvis, tighten your core, allow your head to be free.* Benjamin laughs as I lift and pretend to struggle, "Ooooooh, fat man." Once he's on the bed and we're both free of the straps and transfer mat, the work begins.

I slide Benjamin's pants down a little bit at a time, alternating sides. I ask him to assist me. "Bend your knees, Ben, Ben." There's a lump on the side of his knee, a reminder of the surgically implanted metal plate securing a femur fracture. Benjamin broke his right femur, directly above the knee, twice. The first time he was sitting in his car seat hyperextending his leg. His foot was wedged under the driver's seat directly in front of him. I yelled, "Benjamin, relax! You're going to break your leg."

In the past, I'd helped him release the muscle tension by vibrating his leg as a physical therapist taught me, but I was in the front passenger seat and couldn't position myself to utilize this strategy. I reached for his shin with one hand and pushed his leg, just a bit, to dislodge his foot. He pushed back harder. That's all it took to break the strongest bone in the human body. The orthopedic surgeon urged me not to blame myself. Benjamin's osteoporosis and susceptibility to fracture is not my fault, but I should have known better than to apply any force, no matter how slight, without also providing an appropriate oppositional force. Four weeks in a cast healed the simple fracture. Seven months later, Benjamin suffered a more complex fracture at school during a simple transfer from his wheelchair. When Benjamin suffers, I suffer.

I apply cream to the scar. *Joanne, drop the weight.*

I remove Benjamin's socks and apply more cream to a large scar on the side of his right foot. It's a reminder of the gruesome post-op infection from his second foot surgery. *You can't change it. Just notice.*

Next, I check for any signs of skin breakdown on his right heel. The bone feels too close to the surface after a bedsore depleted the foot's natural cushion during his last hospital stay. I give a slather to the skin covering a bone jutting out of the side of his left foot. Years of wearing orthotics have failed to properly position either foot. Surgery would keep the misaligned bone from causing skin breakdown and infection, but I desperately want to avoid a ninth surgery. *Stay present. Don't give your pain more attention than it deserves.*

Then I remove Benjamin's diaper. When he was born, the only surgical procedure John and I thought we'd need to contemplate was a circumcision. I'm glad we spared him that. I place a pillow between his legs and log roll him onto his side. I apply ointment to the lump on the back of his pelvis, a screw from his scoliosis surgery. A thin line runs the entire length of Benjamin's back. I'm still amazed at how well he recovered from that ten-and-a-half-hour surgery. *Yes, appreciate all that works well.*

I place my hands on Benjamin's back to feel his lungs. Ever since he had pneumonia, we use nebulizer treatments and clap his chest and back to keep his lungs as clear as possible. What would have happened if I hadn't brought him to the emergency room? If I hadn't convinced the GI we were missing something? I fear the day my voice is silenced. *Breathe into this pain. If you don't breathe, you die.*

When I roll Benjamin onto his back, I cannot ignore his asymmetry. The scoliosis surgery straightened him out, but after years of monitoring his dislocating hip, we could not deny the way he winced during every transition and diaper change. The orthopedist planned to perform a bilateral hip adjustment, but Benjamin's bones were too fragile. Unilateral surgery left one leg shorter than the other. His right side is crimped. His ribs just about touch his pelvis. As I place a new pull-up and pajama bottoms, I see the faint lines on his legs and abdomen from his first tendon-lengthening surgery.

I slide Benjamin's shirt up toward his armpits. Despite the second tendon-lengthening surgery, he holds his arms tight up against his body, bent at the elbow, leaving his hooked hands resting on his chest. Benjamin began wearing hand splints when he was just a few months old. Splints could not keep him from tucking his thumbs into his palms. Every year his hands fold tighter. The orthopedist once mentioned surgery to straighten out his wrists. Skillfully broken bones held in place by metal plates won't fix the root of Benjamin's problems.

Benjamin's previous orthopedic surgeon referred to him as "the tin man." As the years pass, my muscles grow more rigid too, and it raises a conflict within me. How long can I do this? Touching one elbow at a time, I ask, "Lift this arm, okay?" When I feel a release, I pull and wrestle the sleeves over his arms. I cradle his head to remove the shirt and tease him until a clean shirt is in place, "Benjamin, you have stinky armpits." *His laughter sends me higher than any suspension.*

There's a barely noticeable line on the left side of Benjamin's upper lip. Now that the cycles of mystery pain are gone, it's the only reminder of the fall he took when John forgot to secure Benjamin's feeding chair lap belt. The plastic surgeon did a wonderful job. John's broken spirit didn't heal quite as seamlessly. *Even though Benjamin has many fragile parts, he is a strong whole. Don't view him by his limitations. View him by who he is on the inside.*

I spread a special cream on the skin around his feeding button. The button has allowed us to feed Benjamin by tube when he refuses to eat pureed food by mouth. He never has to swallow another pill. It's improved his constipation. We can keep him hydrated and fed during illness. But I still hate it. *It's not about you. It's about the process, not the outcome. This intervention improved his quality of life.*

Finally, I strap a triangular pillow between Benjamin's legs to discourage his hips from further dislocation. If ever I felt like my son was a porcelain doll, it was during the six weeks following hip surgery. Every diaper change caused pain. He couldn't sit or tolerate enough tube feedings. The home-based physical therapy was the only support we qualified for. With John at work, I was on my own dealing with Benjamin's physical pain and Sebastian hiding in the garage every time Benjamin cried. Sebastian asked me every day, "When can we send the hospital bed back?"

"Everything will be back to normal soon," I told him. *For every fall there is a recovery.*

I grab the hospital pads under Benjamin and slide him to the middle of his queen size bed, check the position of the pillows under his head, legs, and feet, then prop a small pillow under each elbow. I toss the blanket over his entire body. "Where's Benjamin? There he is," I say, folding the covers across his chest. I turn on the Teletubbies music and line up his stuffed cats and rabbits. Benjamin's eyes grow wide, and his voice croaks with delight. I make the four stuffed Teletubbies perform a dance I choreographed fourteen years ago. They each give Benjamin a kiss before landing in a visible spot on the bed. I switch on the starfish night-light to project an underwater illusion on the ceiling and turn off his lamp. I lean in and cover him with kisses. "I'll see you in the morning." He laughs. "Give Mommy a kiss." He opens his mouth wide as I place my cheek next to his lips. I look into Benjamin's eyes and tell him, "I love you." He replies, "Ahhhh, Laaaaa." Before leaving the room, I pause in his doorway for one last look and say, "Momma loves Ben." If, one day, he doesn't wake, I want those to be the last words he hears.

I have stared into Benjamin's eyes more than I've ever looked into anyone's. There is nothing but here and now and a love unlike any other. His happiness is my happiness. I have learned to embrace the conflicts of motherhood with brutal honesty. All of these experiences make Benjamin Benjamin. They make me his mother. I don't actually want to see my son take his last breath. I don't want to know life without him. For as long as I live, I will do whatever I can to keep Benjamin healthy and give him the best possible quality of life. He is no less than anyone else. He deserves every right and consideration. As Benjamin's advocate, I can guarantee a strong proactive force. When I'm gone, I can do no more. I have no doubt that standing on Benjamin's grave will be more painful than anything I've experienced, but there will be no peace if he is wheeled across mine.

Reach Out and
Trust You Will Find Them

And a time to every purpose under the heaven

Dancing taught me that there's a delicate balance between appreciating life and acting like every second is too precious. Each movement is important and requires equal focus because collectively they strive to express something or produce a reaction, but to fulfill the dance, the participants both on and off the stage can't treat the movement like a fragile gem stored away in a velvet box. Not every individual gesture is memorable. When you create a dance and allow it to take its own natural course, the valuable moments find themselves. There are some things we don't have the power to choose.

Just prior to the semester when I learned *Time*, after years of friendship and relying on each other to lament about our love lives, John and I had a summer fling. One day he stopped returning my phone calls. I'd left him three messages before I realized he was avoiding me. He knew I wasn't looking for a committed relationship, so I didn't appreciate him treating me like a stalking ex-girlfriend. It was beyond me why he was being such a jerk, but

I wasn't worried. I trusted our connection and knew he'd call me when he was ready.

A few months later, John did call asking permission to come see me perform *There Is a Time.* I was feeling rather smug when I said, "Of course you can." While it was nice to have assessed the situation correctly, it was even better to have my friend back and to begin rebuilding a platonic partnership that would grow into something much more than I anticipated. John knew, before I did, where we were heading, which is why he initially got spooked. I'm glad *Time* brought us back together.

When John and I received our tickets to parenthood, we found imperfect seats. The view is extreme and distorted. When I can't understand what is before me, I extend beyond the confines of my mind and reach for the hand of the man who has been beside me for the last thirty-three years. Parenting Benjamin and Sebastian has taken us on a most unimaginable journey. Together we rise, fall, and rise again.

Our past, with all its twists and turns, lives in a collection of pictures, childhood memorabilia, love letters, and school records. When my memory isn't good enough, I escape to our damp, smelly basement to resurrect who I once was. Buried within no fewer than one hundred stacked boxes, there is a dance journal I kept for Jim's Limón technique class. I remember purposely choosing a small, tan, linen-covered notebook. It was easy to identify in any pile. Even at the time, I recognized the journey would be a life-changing event. I read through the journal every now and then. I watch my younger self, in a divided state of performer and audience member, on the now-grainy videocassette copy of the Hunter College Dance Company performing *There Is a Time.*

In the opening circle, the women appear to be dressed in simple, ankle-length, cream-colored dresses. Ample material allowed for a wide, free-flowing dress without revealing the front slit running the full length of the skirt. The neckline of the zippered, form-fitted torso closed with strings tied in a bow, creating a scooped neckline. Throughout the dance, the costume allowed for simple variations. For "War," the women opened the bow and affixed the strings to ties inside the sleeves, thus creating shorter sleeves and a V-neck. A front corner of the skirt was looped through an elastic band on the waistline, giving the dress a narrow, layered effect.

Hunter College borrowed the *Time* costumes from The Juilliard School where Limón first choreographed *Time*. There was something magical about performing at the Hunter College Playhouse, where greater dancers had graced the stage before me, and wearing costumes that had already lived the dance. The costume provided by Juilliard for my "Laugh" solo was too petite. At the time, I felt embarrassed by my size and disappointed to miss out on wearing a piece of history. At five foot five inches and roughly 120 pounds, I was by no means fat, but all these years later, it seems like a defining moment. I didn't fit the mold of a classically trained dancer destined for the Limón Company.

In the last section of the dance, the women were supposed to wear the dresses in the same configuration as the opening circle, in the simplest free-flowing form. Because we had limited male dancers, some of the women assumed larger roles. We weren't able to convert our dresses because we were onstage for the last three sections: War, Peace, and the Closing Circle. At the end of *Time*, I was still dressed for "War." After a final run-through, I happened to be in the audience with Jim and witnessed a moment of panic. "The dresses aren't the same."

He hadn't foreseen the problem until we'd performed in costume. The José Limón Dance Foundation had approved every detail of this reconstruction. Some company members even came to see our run-through. Would this irregularity be acceptable?

Jim quickly dismissed the issue. "It's fine. I like the idea of show-ing the different variations."

At the time, I thought Jim simply chose not to worry about a detail he couldn't change. His decision takes on a new meaning now. Life isn't neatly packaged and beautiful all the time, nor is it in a constant state of disarray. The costumes showed an authentic spectrum of life where extremes coexist.

Now I can appreciate that I'd experienced this lesson on the day my father died as I sat in church breathing in the cold, holy air infused with my brother John's wedding vows and my moth-er's echoing cries. Life is lived simultaneously in love and grief. After mass, my brother Joseph brought me to his apartment. I had torn a hole in my underarm seam. His wife took to the task of mending it. I stripped down to my undergarments, desperate to have this hole pieced back together. Although I was nowhere near puberty, I took cover between the wall and the end of a bookcase. As I waited there in the living room corner, I was able to temporarily hide from the fact that grown-ups can't fix every-thing. Some holes aren't mendable.

I have no memories of the reception. My mother didn't go. The pictures I have seem typical except for a few affectless faces. My maternal grandmother looks serious, frozen between strength and sorrow. I have seen this look in many photos of my Italian ancestors. I look happy in my brother's wedding photos. I suppose I was too young to understand the permanence of death. Perhaps, as children often are, I was easily distracted. I marvel at the image of the little girl on the dance floor, standing on the feet of her new sister in-law's father. I can imagine how pity must have hung heavy in the room. All those eyes watching the youngest, the only daughter on the dance floor with no mother in sight, no father to hold.

I've spent a considerable amount of my life afraid of death. Catholic school taught me to believe death is the beginning of an eternal hereafter where I will reunite with dead loved ones, but even at my father's wake, I found it difficult to lean on this idea. My brother James tried to comfort me as I stared at my father in the casket. He said, "Daddy's having a ball in heaven." My concrete logical, nine-year-old brain conjured up an image of a younger, athletic version of my father playing soccer. It didn't make sense to me then, but I didn't question God's existence.

Religion offers community, rote ceremony, and a predictable structure. Dance gave me a visceral sense of a higher power. During a performance at the Smithsonian, I sat backstage watching a fellow dancer execute simple yet grand movements. The beauty came from the intensity of her execution. The dance, set to a Negro spiritual, was already deep with emotion. As the music streamed through the pianist and his notes carried the dancer, I felt an unearthly presence. Through a rendition of such a dark history, these artists filled me with lightness and hope. I had an undeniable pure belief in the mystery and miracle of life here and beyond. The song still plays in my memory like a lonely somber ghost. We can't run from history or dodge destiny.

On the Internet, I saw a picture of a grave with a statue depicting a child rising up out of his wheelchair and reaching toward heaven. When children like Benjamin die, people like to say, "Now he's running around free of disability." I can no longer strive to cling to this illusion. My sons taught me the dangers of looking too far ahead. I believe this relentless demand to stay present was the final blow to whatever lingering faith I had. I made the choice to relinquish my faith rather than be angry with God. I still live by the moral teachings of Catholicism, but not for the promise of an everlasting life.

Without a belief in God, what is the purpose of all of this? Why did my father die when I was nine? Why did I limit myself, against Jim's advice, to Limón? Why did I leave dance and waste all my time, talent, and Jim's lessons? Why did I become a special educator and then have two children with disabilities? How do I see my journey as anything other than driven by divine intervention?

I've decided that, in order to live a happy, fulfilling life, I need to make my own connections. By linking experiences, I create my own purpose and limit regret. I assign meaning so nothing in my life is wasted. Connecting dance, special education, and parenting has taught me that experiences are multilayered and life lessons are transferable. I no longer lament over the consequences of limiting myself to Limón because now I'm expanding my talent beyond the confines of dance. Sometimes the thought of eternal nothingness does terrify me. I will be ecstatic if the moment after I take my last breath, I find myself in front of Saint Peter at the entrance of the pearly gates, but that's not what drives or comforts me in this life.

There is an organic way to move through space and time. Nature has a way of creating astonishing paths. I love to watch a leaf lilting on a gentle breeze. Its course is completely unpredictable yet oddly serene. Great forces strip a leaf from the branch that secured it to the earth. Though by traditional thought already dead, the wind gives the illusion of life in flight. When it returns to the soil, it completes its intended course.

I fell in love with the Limón technique because it emulates nature's ebb and flow. The dancer uses breath as a means to drive the body. It plays the body like an orchestra. Each body part has a unique voice necessary to fulfill the score. The movements are sequential. Oppositional forces maintain support and control, even when you're off axis. When I imagine myself as nothing more than a simple part of nature, I lose all anxiety and appreciate the unpredictability of life.

"To every thing there is a season, and a time to every purpose under the heaven." In the last section of *Time*, the entire cast came together for the first time since the opening and formed a tight, disconnected circle. One by one we peeled off in a backward spin, expanding the circle while reaching out for each other's hands. Allowing the breath to lead the movement, we widened our chests and sent our collective focus up toward heaven. In rehearsal, Jim had been stern. "Do not look at each other when grasping hands. Just reach out and trust you will find them." Jim was not the type to demonstrate frustration, so when he raised his voice that day, I took note. His words still speak to me. Jim was my mentor because he taught me more than how to be a dancer. He taught me how to live. The best teachers help you ask new questions and lead you to self-discovery. They don't answer every question. They guide.

Time ended as it began, with thirteen dancers standing connected in one large circle center stage. The slow melody of stringed instruments faded. I'd completed the complicated steps. My mind rested. It was good to be finished and yet somewhat sad. There was no going back. The music, psalm, and dance had determined this passage. There was nothing more. So I breathed. Silence fell upon us as we returned to a calm in the aftermath of all that had come before. Every individual was a part of a larger whole. No one dancer bore a greater joy or heavier burden. Everyone and everything was necessary to reveal and balance the central themes of life. So it will continue to be. The lights faded, and I swayed with my fellow dancers soaked in sweat and gratitude. Even in the darkness, our exhausted hands held firm, for together all things were survivable.

Acknowledgments

My deepest thanks to Judith Lindbergh and Michelle Cameron for creating an amazing community of teachers and writers. Without The Writers Circle, this book never would have happened. Special thanks to Paula Balzer, Laurie Lico Albanese, Lisa Romeo, Vinessa Anthony, and the late Sondra Gash for helping me to develop as a writer and making the very arduous process of creating a memoir a joyful one. Thank you to Arielle Eckstut and David Henry Sterry for your support and strong belief that this book would one day be published.

Tina Manfredi, years ago you said, "Write that book of yours." Thank you for saying what I needed to hear at just the right time. Aelish Evers McLeer, thank you for reading my early pages in a school parking lot and "crying big, Lucille Ball tears." I love you like a sister. Without you and Debbie Leardi, this journey would have been so much harder.

To Brenda Considine, who has championed all of my work. Thank you for the opportunities you've given me. Your support and friendship have been an incredible gift. To Connie and Peter Tripi, thank you for spending every Saturday night with us after we first moved to New Jersey and many subsequent evenings since. There's nothing better than good friends, home-cooked meals, and laughter. Connie, my life is so much better because you're in it. Can you hear me screaming? It's pure happiness.

Claire Monaghan, thank you for luring me to West Orange and supporting me personally and professionally. Thank you to the West Orange community for giving my family a true sense of belonging. To every teacher and therapist who partnered with us, thank you for embracing my boys and working ridiculously hard to lead them toward success. To my friends everywhere who have supported my family and this writing dream of mine, thank you.

Thank you to our physicians, especially Dr. Demetrios Gabriel, Dr. Michael Gabriel, Dr. Christina Carter, Dr. Joshua Hyman, Dr. Philip Kazlow, Dr. Orrin Devinsky, Dr. David Feldman, Dr. Eric Geller, and the late Dr. Arnold Gold for taking such beautiful care of our boys. I must give a special thanks to Sophia Mamakas. I would be lost in a mountain of medical paperwork without your support.

To my friends and professors at Hunter College, thank you for giving me some of the best years of my life. Immense gratitude to Billy Siegenfield, Jana Feinman, and the late Jim Clinton. The sixth floor of Thomas Hunter Hall will forever live in my heart, and so will you all. To my Limón teachers, especially Carla Maxwell, Risa Steinberg, Nina Watt, Roxane D'Orleans Juste, Bambi Anderson, and Steuart Gold, thank you for sharing your knowledge and hearts.

Thank you to She Writes Press for saying yes and believing in my ability to tell this story in my own way. Brooke Warner, Jennifer Caven, and Shannon Green, your guidance truly made this process so special.

To my mom, who gave me everything I ever needed to live this life, you have always been my inspiration. To my brothers Joseph, John, Anthony, and especially James. I am so lucky to have your love and support. To my sister-in-law Monica, who has listened to me talk about this book for years and read my earliest pages, I am so grateful for our bond. To Rufina, thank you for your love and kindness. I've always appreciated seeing my

Acknowledgments

boys through your lens. Jacquie, Lisa, Nina, Marie, Betty, Mario, and Tony, I so wish you could be here to celebrate this with me. Dad, nine years wasn't enough time with you. You are loved and missed every day.

All my love and gratitude goes to my husband, John, whose first reaction upon learning I was writing a memoir was, "Be honest. Even if it's painful. I don't care how I look. It's harder to be truthful, but that is what will make it interesting. Don't protect me or anyone. I can handle it." You are the most generous human being, and I am so fortunate to spend my life with you. Thank you for standing by me.

Most of all, to Benjamin and Sebastian. It is quite impossible to explain how much I love you both. I can only hope you have felt my love for you every day. You are two of the most amazing people I have ever known. Thank you for your love and your perfect way of being.

About the Author

Joanne De Simone is a graduate of Hunter College with degrees in dance and special education. After dancing professionally with companies including José Limón and Dianne McIntyre, she dedicated her life to teaching children with disabilities and supporting their families. Currently, Joanne is a special education advocate for the Alliance of Private Special Education Schools of North Jersey. Her writing has appeared in the *Washington Post*, *Exceptional Parent Magazine*, and the *Rumpus*, among other publications. She is a contributing author to *Barriers and Belonging: Personal Narratives of Disability*. Joanne and her son Sebastian were instrumental in a legislative change allowing students with intellectual disabilities to participate in NCAA D3 intercollegiate sports. Joanne has been featured in the *Philadelphia Inquirer*, on *HuffPost Live*, *CNN*, and *GMA3*. Visit www.Special-EducationMom.com for more information.

Looking for your next great read?

We can help!

Visit www.shewritespress.com/next-read
or scan the QR code below for a list
of our recommended titles.

She Writes Press is an award-winning
independent publishing company founded to
serve women writers everywhere.